Sept 29, 1995

Guy - Merry 40th

Love, Joan & Kr.

The Amana People and Their Furniture

The Amana People and Their Furniture

Marjorie K. Albers

Iowa State University Press / Ames

Marjorie K. Albers, formerly an assistant professor in interior design at the University of Nebraska-Lincoln, more recently has been a practicing interior designer. She lives near Iowa City, Iowa.

© 1990 Iowa State University Press, Ames, Iowa 50010
All rights reserved

Manufactured in the United States of America
⊛ This book is printed on acid-free paper.

First edition, 1990

Library of Congress Cataloging-in-Publication Data
Albers, Marjorie K.
    The Amana people and their furniture / Marjorie K. Albers.— 1st ed.
        p.   cm.
    Includes bibliographical references and index.
    ISBN 0-8138-1239-9.—ISBN 0-8138-1238-0 (pbk.)
    1. Furniture, Amana.   2. Amana Society.   3. Furniture—Iowa—History.
I. Title.
NK2435.I8A4   1990
749.2177'653—dc20   90-43783

To the people of the seven Amana villages

Contents

Preface

Amana has always meant something special to me. My great-grandmother and great-grandfather, great-uncle and great-aunt, and grandfather came to Amana when they first arrived in this country from Mecklenburg, Germany, in the late 1860s. Although they did not become members of the Society, they lived and worked in Amana for several years.

As a child, I lived a short distance from the seven villages and remember the many visits with my parents to homes—the striped rag carpeting on the floors, the gliders in the yards, the sauerkraut, and the beautiful walnut chests and chairs in airy rooms with blue walls.

As the years go by, the Amana of an earlier era is changing. Only the descendants and friends can relate the living word of the immediate past. The human tie continues, but this link will gradually weaken. I owe a debt of gratitude to those who have helped me, many of whom are recognized in the acknowledgments. Wouldn't it have been nice to have had an interview with my great-grandfather? I consider it a privilege to have played a part in the making of a historical record of the people of Amana and their furniture.

Acknowledgments

I wish to express gratitude to the many individuals who have helped in numerous ways to compile the historical and current data that are the bases for this book. The people of the seven historic villages have been most generous in opening their hearts, homes, and businesses to tell me their story.

Marvin A. Bendorf, a native of Amana, has ably served as an advisor to me in the development of this book. Mr. Bendorf is a graduate of the University of Iowa. He taught in the Iowa school system, was employed by Amana Refrigeration for a time, and was manager of the Amana Furniture Shop for thirty years. He has served on the State Board of the Center for Industrial Research and Service at Iowa State University (CIRAS), the Amana Society Board of Directors, and Amana church Board of Trustees. He was an Elder for twenty-five years. His background and experience in the furniture industry of Amana enabled him to provide valuable information and insights.

Peter A. Krumhardt took all of the photos except those from the photographic collections of the Amana Heritage Society, the State Historical Society of Iowa, and Amana Refrigeration, Inc. He is a staff photographer at the Iowa State University Photo Service. He came to Iowa from Illinois and is a graduate of Iowa State University. In addition to his full-time position, Krumhardt is a free-lance photographer, primarily of horticultural subjects, and pursues woodworking as a hobby.

While it is impossible to give due credit to all who have contributed in their respective ways, I would like to extend my appreciation to Arthur Barlow, Henry A. Bendorf, Jr., Marvin and Emaline Bendorf, Adolph Berger, Daniel Berger, Dean and Donna Berger, Adam Clemens, Erna Noe Conrow, Elmer Dittrich, Erma Fels, George Foerstner, H. C. Geiger, Leonard Graf, Lanny Haldy, Barbara Hoehnle, Ann Humbert, Rudolph and Erma Kellenberger, Theo and Helen Kippenhan, Marcelee Konish, Rudy Kraft, Walter and Erika Kraft, Marvin Krauss, Henry and Henrietta Moershel, Cathy Oehl, H. W. Pitz, David Rettig, Ferdinand and Henrietta Ruff, Norman and Joanna Schanz, Walter and Florence Schuerer, Walter Seifert, Marie Selzer, Don Shoup, and Connie Zuber. They gave freely of their time to talk with me and let many of their historic and current furnishings be photographed. A number of the above-named individuals also provided information for my first book, *Old Amana Furniture,* a small portion of which has been included in this work. While a few of these have now passed away, their contributions are not forgotten.

I would like to thank Carla Tollefson and other editorial personnel of the Iowa State University Press for their valuable suggestions for improving the content and readibility of my book.

A special thank you to my husband, Henry H. Albers, who translated some original German sources and gave me the advantage of his expertise as an economist. His support and enthusiasm are greatly appreciated.

The Amana People and Their Furniture

CHAPTER 1

Introduction

A long the hillsides and valleys of the Iowa River, twenty miles west of Iowa City, Iowa, are seven villages of nineteenth-century charm. These villages—Amana, Middle Amana, East Amana, South Amana, West Amana, High Amana, and Homestead—are surrounded by twenty-five thousand acres of rich Iowa soil and timberland. They were built and settled by members of the Community of True Inspiration (later known as the Amana Society), people originally from Alsace (France), Germany, and Switzerland who were seeking seclusion from the outside world and its distractions so that they could worship as they pleased. An important part of the community's religion is the belief that some individuals have a gift of inspiration through which they express the will of God. Common aspirations and religious fervor have held this community together for many generations.

In the secular realm, members of the community shared in the work and rewards; an orderly system of communal living prevailed. During the early years, life in Amana had few of the adornments and trappings of the external world. Out of necessity, in 1932 the people chose to change their communal system to a capitalistic one.

It is difficult to recapture the environment of the past. When the Inspirationists made their move from Europe to

Ebenezer, near Buffalo, New York, in the 1840s, and from Ebenezer to Iowa in the middle and late 1850s, much of the United States was still frontier, with large expanses of Indian territory. Iowa was sparsely settled and the land that became Amana had scarcely been disturbed by the plow and the axe. The early Amana villages were traversed by horse and wagon, and oxen were still commonly used to cultivate the soil.

The railroad had not yet arrived in Homestead, the town the Amana Society later purchased. There were no bridges across the Iowa River for the first contingent of Inspirationists. The lack of such infrastructure served, for a time at least, to give these religious people the isolation they so vigorously sought. Eventually modern highways, the automobile, and the radio brought the outside world into their midst.

Throughout the years of its existence Amana has been well known for its fine handcrafted furniture, yet little has been written on the subject. This book was undertaken to tell the story of the move of a group of religious people from Europe to central Iowa, the role furniture played in their lives, and how their furniture-making craft subsequently became an important industry.

Furniture may be defined as the movable and decorative articles within a space that make it inhabitable, comfortable, and artistically pleasing. It occupies a central place in the lives of people and is symbolic of a way of life. The nature of furniture reflects the past, daily life, economic endeavor, and social status, as well as the role of religion in a society. Alan Gowans commented that "architecture and furniture are history in its most tangible form."[1] The strength of this rich heritage is evidenced by the thriving and renowned handcrafted furniture industry found in the Amanas today.

CHAPTER 2

Historical Background

The Inspirationist Movement

During the sixteenth and seventeenth centuries there was considerable religious unrest in central and western Europe. Many sects found fault with the dogmatism and formality of the Lutheran church and felt that the Bible was not given sufficient attention as a source of spiritual inspiration. One small group, the Mystics, was formed by people who "had become wary of the endless disputes about tenets and creeds; they had lost all faith in outward religious profession; they were at last ready to fall back on something deeper and better than mere formality; they wanted 'to worship God in spirit and truth.' "[1] These believers were joined by the Pietists, who under the leadership of Philipp Jacob Spener had become involved in a popular movement that combined the Lutheran emphasis on creed and doctrine with the ideas of the Reformed church on the importance of pious living.

Such were the modest beginnings of the Community of True Inspiration in the German state of Hesse in 1714. Under the leadership of a Lutheran clergyman, Eberhard Ludwig Gruber, and a clergyman's son, Johann Friedrich Rock, the movement had its origin. Rock and Gruber traveled extensively throughout northern Europe and established many small congregations of followers. They often were met by an unfriendly populace and experienced considerable hostility when they arrived in a town or village. It was only in those places where the townspeople were inclined toward some form of Pietism that they were not turned away. Yet their courage and religious fervor did not waiver. William Perkins and Barthinius Wick stated that it was around these two men, Rock and Gruber, " 'their heroes of faith,' that the development and progress of the Community has turned as if on an axis."[2]

It was the belief of the Inspirationists that God spoke to and inspired certain individuals. As Bertha Shambaugh wrote: "Divine guidance came through individuals who were regarded as especially endowed by the Lord with the 'miraculous gift of Inspiration' and who were called *Werkzeuge*."[3] Francis DuVal describes this gift of inspiration:

> Revelation could be presented at any time and in any place, but was most likely to occur during an assembly for worship. There was not, however, any designated time during the worship reserved for it; a revelation sometimes did not take place at all, while often it occurred several times during one service. The instrument frequently became inspired while on a journey or while preaching in the streets; and it was not infrequent that the Lord spoke through the instrument during the night.[4]

The *Werkzeuge* were usually accompanied by scribes who recorded the words of prophecy at the moment of revelation. (These treasured words, serving as a written guide of faith, continue to play a major role in the services of the Amana churches today.)

With the deaths of Gruber in 1728 and Rock in 1749, the movement was left without a *Werkzeug*. Perkins and Wick lauded the contributions of Gruber: "The Society lost its greatest leader, a loss which was never made good. It was Gruber who first collected the little body of believers, who formulated the doctrines of their creed, and who spread those doctrines beyond the boundaries of Germany."[5] Many Inspirationists, especially the younger generation, were gradually attracted to more worldly ways.

The movement declined and membership dwindled.

A reawakening and revival occurred in 1817 when Michael Krausert, a tailor of Strasbourg, renewed the faith and the teachings of Rock and Gruber. Among those reached were Barbara Heinemann, a peasant maid, and Christian Metz, a young Ronneburg carpenter. They are credited with being the strongest forces in the development of the new Communities of True Inspiration in Europe and later in America.

In the face of continuous religious intolerance from church and state, many groups of Inspirationists migrated to the more liberal German state of Hesse. The Ronneburg, a five-hundred-year-old walled castle high on a hilltop, was the first gathering place. In 1826, the brethren were able to lease the Marienborn castle. About this time the lease on the Ronneburg was lost, yet membership was growing. More space was needed. Metz began to assume an increasingly important leadership role and sought to rent additional castles and cloisters. In 1828 he acquired an estate at Herrnhaag (near the Ronneburg) as another refuge for the faithful. In 1832 a cloister was rented at Arnsburg for the Swiss and Alsatian members; it was renamed the Armenburg ("castle of the poor") by the Inspirationists. Soon thereafter a cloister at Engelthal was occupied by members from Württemberg. An attempt was made to accommodate differences in nationalities and customs. All of the sites, except the Armenburg, were within five miles of one another; most could be viewed from the towers of the Ronneburg.

Through cooperative endeavors some communal living began in the estates that were leased. Frank Lankes wrote that "being driven from the 'world' they contributed toward each other's welfare with whatever substance or talent they possessed."[6] It was more practical and profitable for the farmers to work the many acres of land jointly, for some of the women to prepare the food together in a centralized location, and for the artisans to continue in their trades rather than try new ones. Financial contributions for community enterprises were made by some of the wealthy Inspirationists.

As more and more people joined the group, economic pressures grew. Metz, who felt he had the guidance of the

Ronneburg Castle, Hesse, Germany. (Photographic Collection, State Historical Society of Iowa)

Lord, and the Elders rented a woolen mill, a gristmill, and an oil mill. The woolen mill became an especially successful enterprise because of the high quality of materials used and the excellent workmanship. The woven woolens were soon sold throughout the region and became a much-needed source of funds. Products were cooperatively marketed and the proceeds were shared.

Christian Metz, Religious Leader and Cabinetmaker

Christian Metz was born in December 1793 in Neuwied, Germany, into a family of seven children.[7] His father was a tanner by trade, and his mother, though it has not been confirmed, was said to have been of noble birth. Strong religious fervor characterized the members of the Metz family.

A great-grandfather had been directed by a revelation to move to the castle that later was to be known as the Ronneburg and the center of Inspirationist worship and cooperative endeavor.

The immediate family of Christian Metz became residents of the Ronneburg in 1801, where it is thought that Metz received his formal education and religious training. During his teens Metz was greatly influenced by two individuals: an Elder and cabinetmaker to whom he was apprenticed, and a man named Jacob Andres, whose philosophy and religious teachings guided Metz in later years.

Metz's religious mission was important throughout his adult life. The first of more than thirty-six hundred divine inspirations occurred when he was about twenty-six years old. Many of the important decisions made by Metz and the Inspirationists were in response to these divine revelations. Metz played a major role in moving the Inspirationists from Germany to Ebenezer and then to Amana. He formulated and successfully implemented a communal approach to economic endeavor, and from time to time he practiced his trade as a carpenter and cabinetmaker.

Metz's contribution to the Inspirationists during his years in Germany was described by DuVal: "Metz was constantly busy going from one congregation to the next, endeavoring always to give the members faith and confidence through his leadership. At the same time he was making many appearances before the authorities in an effort to defend and justify the cause of the Inspirationists."[8] There was much opposition from the established clergy and governmental officials. Metz and other Inspirationists, both men and women, were often incarcerated in dank and dreary prisons. Congregations were persecuted for refusing to send their children to state-sponsored schools or to take oaths required for legal and other purposes. They objected to and refused military service. The trials and tribulations continued unabated until finally, in 1842, Metz was told in a divine inspiration to seek a new home in America.

In September 1842 a committee of four—Metz; George A. Weber, a physician-surgeon; Wilhelm Noe, a barber-surgeon; and Gottlieb Ackerman, a businessman—departed from Bremen on the ship *New York* for the thirty-six-day voyage. The journey was not easy; hope was buoyed only by the belief that the trip was sanctioned by the Lord. Accommodations on the 120-foot vessel were cramped, the sea was rough, the cabin had to be shared with nonbelievers, and the Inspirationists were without privacy for their twice-daily worship and prayers. There were several bad storms and almost all on board the small ship were seasick for much of the trip. At times during the trip Metz tried to visualize transporting some eight hundred land-loving Inspirationists—the young, the old, the families with their limited but valued possessions— across the wide expanse of the Atlantic.

After a brief stay in New York the committee proceeded by steamer and horse-drawn canal boat to Buffalo, New York, where the Seneca Indian Reservation was perhaps available for purchase. The reservation had been acquired by the Ogden Company of New York, and the Indians were supposed to vacate in two years. There began a long period of negotiations, misunderstandings, pricing problems, and difficulties with the Indians, who were reluctant to leave. After many delays the committee purchased five thousand acres of land for $10.50 an acre. (At this time "beef was a cent a pound and pork two cents, butter ten cents a pound, and flour three dollars and fifty for a barrel of 180 pounds.")[9] When complex legal problems were resolved, a deed was obtained. Additional land was purchased, and the area became known as Ebenezer.

Christian Metz proposed that there be communal ownership in Ebenezer for an initial period of two years. All property, except personal property and household equipment, was to be held in common by the members; the loans were to be repaid with interest to the individual contributors after two years.[10] Food would be provided by community kitchens and paid for out of wages for work performed. Disputes were to be resolved by the Elders. These measures were designed to provide money for the purchase of land, to resolve conflicts over property rights, and to promote cooperation among people of unequal wealth and social status.

In spite of some opposition, Wilhelm Moershel, Carl Winzenried, and G. A. Weber formulated "a constitution

SCHEDULE 1.—Free Inhabitants in _Amana Township_ **in the County of** _Iowa_ **State of** _Iowa_ **enumerated by me, on the** _2d_ **day of** _Aug_ **1860.** _F. Ellig_ **by Asst Marshal.**

Post Office _Homestead_

Dwelling houses numbered in the order of visitation	Families numbered in the order of visitation	The name of every person whose usual place of abode on the first day of June, 1860, was in this family	Age	Sex	Color (White, black, or mulatto)	Profession, Occupation, or Trade of each person, male and female, over 15 years of age.	Value of Real Estate	Value of Personal Estate	Place of Birth, Naming the State, Territory, or County.	Married within the year	Attended School within the year	Persons over 20 y'rs of age who cannot read and write	Whether deaf and dumb, blind, insane, idiotic, pauper, or convict
			4	5	6	7	8	9	10	11	12	13	14
1033	1034	Christian Metz	66	M	W	Cabinet Maker	25,000	5000	Hessen				
		Wm	62	M		Watch Maker			"				
		Anna M. Krames	42	F					Preussen				
		Catharine	15	F									
		Christina	10	F									
		Ludwig Weber	28	M		Blacksmith			Hessen				
		Barbara Oberr	57	F					Baden				
		Amelia Schmitz	17	F					Switzerland				
1035	1037	Barnabas Geyer	61	M		Farmer			Switzerland				
		Anna	53	F									
		Barbara Barkein	69	M		Architect							
		Louis M	32	F					France				

A partial page of the 1860 federal census in which Christian Metz, the Werkzeug, identified himself as a cabinetmaker.

which would perpetuate the concept of communal owner-ship."[11] The approval of God was indicated in several revelations from Metz, giving support for a continuation of the communal system. The constitution was approved in January 1846 by the Elders and the congregations of three villages. The first signature was that of Christian Metz. An act of the New York legislature gave official and legal status to the document. This constitution was essentially the same as that later adopted in Amana.

Only persons who accepted the religious doctrines and secular mandates of the Community of True Inspiration could be admitted to membership. Members were required to deed all money and property, except personal effects, to the community. In some instances the amount was considerable; one member reportedly contributed fifty thousand dollars. Others had little or nothing to give. Full membership and all the rights and privileges relating thereto were formally conferred through the signing of the constitution.

All his life Christian Metz played a major role in the religious and secular life of the Community of True Inspiration. His guidance was especially important in the difficult and often hazardous moves from Germany to Ebenezer and again to Amana. As *Werkzeug* and Elder he was held in high esteem. Yet he revealed his basic sense of humility when he listed his occupation as cabinetmaker in the federal census of 1860.[12]

From Hesse to Ebenezer

The liquidation of community property in Hesse began as soon as it was practical, but many difficulties were encountered. The process was slowed considerably by a major fire that destroyed the highly valued woolen-mill machinery destined for Ebenezer. Great effort was made to settle personal affairs quickly so that the Inspirationists could depart for their new home in America. The first group of fifty people arrived early and unexpectedly, within four months from the time the first steps were taken to purchase land. Such migrations continued between 1843 and 1846 and increased the number of people to eight hundred.

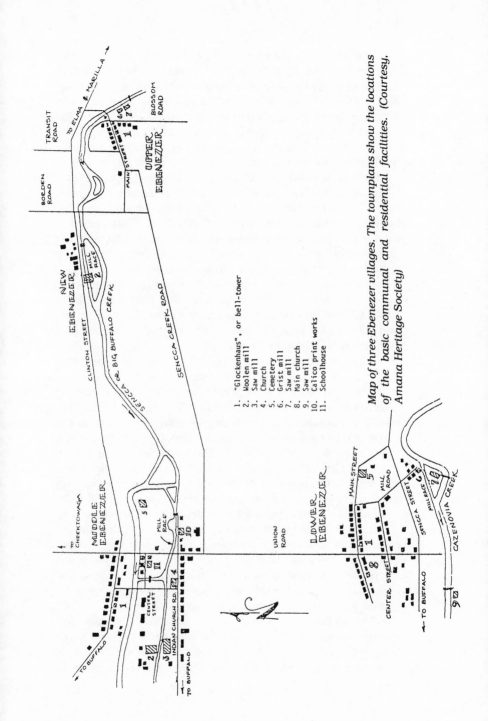

Map of three Ebenezer villages. The townplans show the locations of the basic communal and residential facilities. (Courtesy, Amana Heritage Society)

1. "Glockenhaus", or bell-tower
2. Woolen mill
3. Saw mill
4. Church
5. Cemetery
6. Grist mill
7. Saw mill
8. Main church
9. Saw mill
10. Calico print works
11. Schoolhouse

People were inclined to bring as much of their personal property as manageable—furniture, tools, and equipment. The belongings of one group required the drivers of six wagons to make the trip from Buffalo to Ebenezer twice a day for three days. Some of this furniture and the trunks for the smaller items can be found in Amana homes today.

As the population increased, four villages were established in Ebenezer. The first was Middle or *Mittel* Ebenezer (now Gardenville, New York), followed by Upper or *Ober* Ebenezer (presently Blossom), Lower or *Nieder* Ebenezer (later Ebenezer), and New or *Neu* Ebenezer (the area between Gardenville and Blossom). Within a short period of time a number of Canadians also became members of the Community of True Inspiration. Since some in the group were landowners, the decision was made to establish two more villages on the Canadian land owned by a few of these members. One village was located about forty-five miles northwest of Buffalo and was named Kenneberg. The second village, Canada Ebenezer, was twelve miles north of Buffalo on the Niagara River.

For a period of sixteen years, all the New York property was held in common, and the Community of True Inspiration was constituted a corporate body through legislative enactment of the State of New York. The control of the property, the management of community enterprises, and the responsibility for the welfare of the people were vested in a board of trustees who were also Elders. The Elders planned construction and production activities, and made decisions concerning the lands to be plowed and crops planted. People were assigned to particular locations and directed to labor as was deemed most advantageous to the community.

In spite of all the benefits of cooperative endeavor, the newcomers faced many problems. Stones and trees had to be cleared to create farmland. After the village town plans were laid out, homes, schools, churches, businesses, and mills needed to be built. Roadways and bridges were required for transportation and communication.

The first families moved temporarily into the house formerly occupied by the chief of the Seneca Indians while their own large frame houses were being constructed by members and hired workmen. Clair Watson noted that

Factory in Middle Ebenezer. (Photographic Collection, Amana Heritage Society)

"there is a record of skilled carpenters, masons, and cabinet makers, coming with their tools in the first contingent and that they began immediately to erect dwellings in those new Ebenezer villages near Buffalo."[13] Each of the new structures housed several families; the comfort of the individual families was at all times a prime consideration. The cooking was done in large kitchens and the meals were eaten at a common table.

The practices of these new immigrants differed significantly from those of other pioneers. Everyone lived together in the villages, with the farmland between the villages.

Large groups of fifty or more men, and often women, worked side by side in the fields to harvest grain. The people in surrounding communities were unaccustomed to seeing a shepherd and his dogs tend grazing animals along roadsides and green paths to conserve as much grass and grain as possible.

The "way of life" was strict. A member needed permission from an Elder to go from one village to another. There were no paupers, no criminals, no lawsuits. Nor was anyone dependent on the outside society for support. The final steps toward a more communistic system were taken. Members who had made financial contributions to cover the land purchases and other costs were given noninterest-bearing receipts that provided for the return of principal if the member left the community. Personal belongings remained as private property. All secular day-to-day activity was organized to provide an environment that was conducive to a religious way of life. A considerable amount of time was spent in worship.

As Buffalo grew, the Elders realized that they needed greater isolation if they were to maintain their unity and religious ideals. Shambaugh observed that "the thriving city of Buffalo with its worldly influences and attractions was too easily accessible to the young people for the peace of mind of the Elders, who considered the salvation of the soul of paramount importance in this world."[14] In addition to religious considerations, the idea of moving west to new lands was prompted by several factors: the antagonism that had developed in the surrounding towns toward the Inspirationists, a reduction in available water power for mill operation as the result of industrial growth in Buffalo, the probability that a railroad extension might be laid through community property, and the possible expiration of a land lease.

The city of Buffalo was expanding toward the Ebenezer villages. Word had spread about the comfortable life-style of the non-Inspirationist German immigrants living in Buffalo and how they were able to save money and enjoy many luxuries. The reports caused some members to leave and tempted others. All of these conditions convinced the Elders and members alike that relocation to the more isolated frontier lands was essential. The frontier to the west was a possible solution. Inspirations of the *Werkzeuge*, Christian Metz and Barbara Heinemann, provided divine approval for a move. The search began in September 1854 when a small committee traveled by steamboat and stage from Buffalo to Kansas, a land that had recently been opened for settlement. This committee had sent an introductory letter to the governor, who in response traveled a considerable distance to greet the Inspirationists and express his interest in having the community settle in the

Schlosseri, *or locksmith's workshop, in Middle Ebenezer. (Photographic Collection, Amana Heritage Society)*

state. The Indians of the area were friendly and favorably impressed the men from Ebenezer. However, much of the land had too little surface water and timber. Periodic prairie fires and the nightly howls of coyotes were further deterrents. The strenuous trip ended in indecision, and no land was purchased.[15]

In December 1854 two men, Johannus Beyer and Jacob Wittmer, were dispatched to look for land in Iowa. They traveled to the westernmost point of the railroad, Davenport, Iowa, then by riverboats on the Mississippi and the Iowa rivers to Iowa City, the capital of the state. Iowa City was where the "land agents flourished and where the boomers grew rich in the practice of their trade."[16] The last leg of the journey to Amana, a segment of only eighteen miles, was made by way of the Iowa City–Des Moines stagecoach. The travelers were impressed with the countryside that lay before them.

From Ebenezer to Amana

The Iowa land was beautiful and largely untouched by civilization. The terrain and natural resources appeared to be suitable and to be able to fulfill expectations. The committee liked the quiet seclusion of the Iowa River valley and adjacent prairie and woodlands, where they felt that "they could practice the doctrines of their creed undisturbed, and carry on communism without coming in contact with the rest of mankind."[17]

The committee of two returned to *Mittel* Ebenezer on December 23, 1854, with the details of a successful search. On December 25, 1854, the *Bruderrat* met in the home of Carl Winzenried, and in a revelation to Christian Metz, the Lord gave guidance that the community should move to this new place called Iowa.[18] On January 25, 1855, a subsequent revelation advised them that they should follow the example of the bees and gather all their possessions in one place. Four days later, January 29, 1855, the Elders began developing a financial plan for the purchase of land in Iowa. A committee of four—Carl Winzenried, Frederick Heinemann, Jacob Wittmer, and Johannus Beyer—left on May

31, 1855, for Iowa to begin the real estate transactions. Metz instructed that outlying land should be purchased prior to any tracts adjacent to proposed village sites, a measure designed to keep costs low. Although virgin lands could be purchased from the government for $1.25 an acre, the agents representing the Inspirationists paid a significantly higher price for cleared and ready-to-plant land. In one instance a farm consisting of eleven hundred acres was purchased for an average price of $11.48 an acre from Charles and Newell Whiting.[19] (Reference is still made to the Whiting farm when the Amana Society assigns farm workers.) By mid-1855 arrangements had been made for the purchase of a sizable body of fertile Iowa farmland that was to become Amana; the holding ultimately consisted of some twenty-six thousand acres.

There are two ways to settle a frontier. One is through the arrival of individual families in a more or less haphazard fashion. During the early years, such pioneers often experienced extreme loneliness and much hardship. They would not see a human face outside of their own family for months on end. Housing was primitive and food scarce. One pioneer family in Iowa County, the county in which the Inspirationists settled, had nothing to eat for weeks but baked squash, wild game, and a few fish.[20]

The second way to settle a frontier is that of the Inspirationists, which was to move a complete society and build the necessary infrastructure through organized endeavor over a relatively short span of time. The Ebenezer Inspirationists moved to the Iowa frontier and settled in their Iowa villages with new homes, churches, schools, and business enterprises within approximately ten years—1855 to 1865.

The Move Westward

The move from Ebenezer to Iowa was well planned and accomplished without financial loss. Christian Metz and the Elders decided that one group of members, those with agricultural and construction skills, would be the first to go west; the others would remain in Ebenezer until the land was sold. However, the leaders did not foresee that selling the land would be as slow and difficult as it was. Each of the villages had mills, factories, and a cluster of houses and farm buildings nestled together, with tillable land and timberland in between. The straight-lined post-and-board fences of the conservative German community had replaced the picturesque split-log zigzag fences of Cayuga Creek. Potential buyers were unaccustomed to such an arrangement of property. Letters from George Weber in New York, one of the three in whom the Elders had conveyed the authority to sell Ebenezer lands, reflected "the desolation that he experienced as outsiders re-settled the colony. Large auctions were held at intervals and quantities of tools, livestock, household furnishings, etc. were sold."[21]

Thirty-three members made up the first group; it left for Iowa on July 9, 1855, and included people from each of the Ebenezer villages—mainly farmers, carpenters, masons, and others necessary for the orderly development of the first Amana villages. This group, as many of the subsequent groups who followed at appropriate intervals, took equipment and supplies, leaving an adequate inventory of such items for those who remained. The ten-day trip to Iowa was frequently arduous, especially during the months when snow was deep and temperatures low. Spring rains caused rivers to flood. Food supplies were limited. The difficult conditions caused insecurity and uncertainty, all of which led to reduced compatibility and cooperation. Metz made many trips between Ebenezer and Amana but felt compelled to write frequent letters of encouragement and guidance to the Inspirationists in both locations. Within a decade, approximately eight hundred members had moved westward by essentially the same route.

In the years before the railroad to Homestead was completed (1860), personal and household items were moved "by steamboat to Chicago, and from there by rail to Davenport, from which place they had to go by stage direct to Homestead."[22] Barbara Hoehnle notes, "The church had transported benches all the way from Germany and just reassembled the benches with pegs. This process was repeated twelve years later when the Community began the migration to Iowa."[23] Marjorie Wightman wrote that the "transporting of weaving looms, farm implements and

furniture had been one of the community's most compli-
cated problems."[24] Some Amana families still possess large
wooden moving chests made by their forefathers; the New
York–Homestead address is clearly marked on the outside.

The name initially given to the new settlement in Iowa
was *Bleibtreu*, as set forth in a song that came as an inspiration to Christian Metz on August 8, 1855.[25] The song begins
Bleibtreu soll der Name sein Dort in Iowa, der Gemein.
Since the wording did not seem appropriate in English
translation, the name Amana was selected and given approval in a second song that came through inspiration on
September 23, 1855.[26] The word *Amana*, which translates
from Hebrew as "constant," appears in the Song of Solo-
mon in the Bible and has a meaning similar to that of *Bleibtreu.*

The Inspirationists were pleased with their new home
in Iowa. The quiet, rural acres provided an ideal setting in
which they could practice their religion and live undisturbed by outsiders. All that had been risked and sacrificed
for more than a century was brought into focus on the Iowa
prairie. The success of the future was dependent on the unity, willingness to work, and religious faith of these people.

Christian Metz died on July 27, 1867, six years after
the establishment of the last of the seven villages. The here-
tofore relatively inactive Barbara Heinemann[27] carried on
alone as *Werkzeug* until her death in 1883. Since that time
there have been no other *Werkzeuge* to directly relate the
will of the Lord; only the *Bezeugungen* (revelations/inspira-
tions) from the past remain for solace and edification.[28]

CHAPTER 3

The Amana Villages

The Iowa Countryside

The search committee had made an excellent choice in recommending Iowa as the new home of the Community of True Inspiration. Natural resources were abundant. There were acres of nearly contiguous prairie land, some flat and some rolling. The flat land was ideal for growing agricultural crops; the rolling slopes and hillsides were chosen for village sites. The prairie did not require the removal of trees and stones, as had been the case in Ebenezer. The soil was fertile and suitable for the growing of barley, potatoes, corn, oats, wheat, tobacco, onions, broomcorn, and other crops. Oxen could soon be pulling the plows and wagons, and cattle and sheep grazing on the grassy slopes.

There was an adequate supply of water for power and palate. The Iowa River flowed through the central part of the area, a factor important in locating the villages close to one another. Of lesser importance were Price Creek on the northern border, the English River and its tributaries, the Cedar River, and a segment of Old Man's Creek. The water level was sufficiently high so that most of the community residents could have a hand pump in the house yard to supply household water needs. Artesian water was available in the area that was to become known as Upper South Amana.

Oxen used for farm operations. (Photographic Collection, State Historical Society of Iowa)

Timberlands were situated along the banks, on the bluffs, and in the valleys of the rivers and streams. There was a plentiful supply of hickory, walnut, oak, willow, birch, elm, green ash, pine, and butternut trees. A great many of the community houses, barns, and other buildings would be of wood frame construction; making furniture and wagons would require large amounts of wood. It was also important as fuel.

In locating the villages, consideration was given to the proximity of other natural resources used in the building process—sandstone, clay, and limestone. Closeness would reduce the time and costs usually incurred obtaining and transporting such building materials. Sandstone was found along the Iowa River near West Amana and adjacent to Amana and East Amana. It could be quarried for the foundations of houses and barns, and in some instances for the exteriors of meetinghouses, schools, and homes. Clay was available for making bricks.

23

The beautiful and peaceful countryside of the Iowa prairie seemed ideal for the new home of the Inspirationists. The abundance of good land, water, and building materials within the area would help the members meet their physical needs; the isolation and tranquility could provide a much-desired setting for them to meet their religious needs. The wisdom and guidance of Christian Metz would once again lead the members of the Community of True Inspiration to a land that was to serve them well.

The Seven Villages

The plan the Inspirationists used in laying out their new communities in Iowa was similar to the plan they had developed in Ebenezer, where several decentralized villages had been established as a means of enforcing discipline and having a suitable distribution of population and farmland. The settlers would once again live in small villages three to four miles apart, about one hour away by oxen. As the families arrived, six villages were established, each assuming the name of Amana and a prefix describing the location in relation to the first village, which was known as Amana. East Amana was east of the first colony, Middle Amana was centrally located, and so on with West Amana, High Amana, and South Amana. An additional settlement was located approximately one-half mile south of South Amana along the roadbed of the Chicago, Milwaukee, St. Paul, and Pacific Railroad; while it was known as Upper South, it was considered a part of South Amana. Later, the names of these villages became shortened. Each was known by the prefix—East Amana became East, West Amana became West, and so on.[1] The town of Homestead was purchased in 1861 because it was the westernmost shipping point of the Mississippi and Missouri Railway, which later became known as the Chicago, Rock Island, and Pacific Railroad.

Each village, as in Ebenezer, was laid out with one long primary street and several short parallel streets cutting off to the right and left. The factories and workshops were at one end of the main street and the barns and sheds at the other. There was no business district as such. The churches

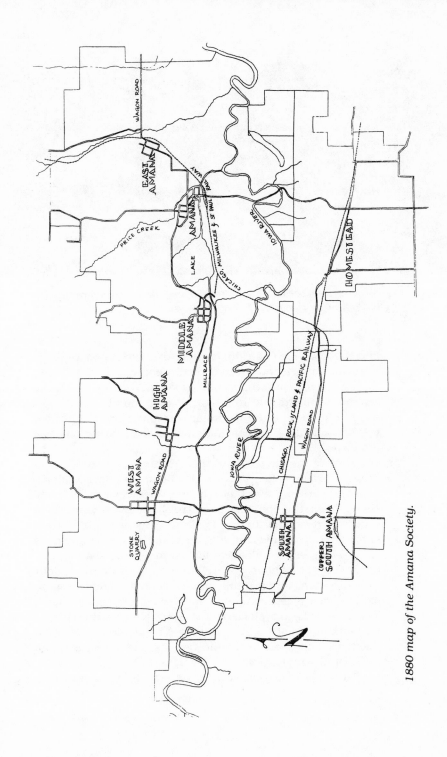

1880 map of the Amana Society.

Amana street scene. All buildings looked alike. (Photographic Collection, State Historical Society of Iowa)

and schools were centrally located, the communal kitchens were numerous and interspersed among the other buildings, and each community had a lookout fire tower atop the building housing the fire-fighting equipment. Residences were built close to the workplaces of the men who headed the households. Between the villages were farmlands and forests.

Most of the villages had their own general stores, bakeries, dairies, wagon shops, coopershops, forges, locksmiths, wine cellars, tailor shops, medical offices, shoe shops, basket shops, and blacksmith shops. A sawmill in each village served the needs of the carpentry and cabinet shops. Areas of endeavor with a limited demand had shops in only one or two villages: for example, the soap works, lumberyard, tin shops, umbrella shops, watchmakers, flour mill, plumbing and printing shops, machine shops, harness shops, bookbinderies, starch factory, and broom makers. There were grain elevators, granaries, brick kilns, and woolen mills in strategic locations. The general stores supplied the needs of the Inspirationists and in some cases those of nearby Iowa County farmers.

Amana, the largest village, was the first colony to be

26

settled (1855). By 1900 the population was 550. The calico print mill, built about 1860, quickly grew to be a flourishing village enterprise with a broad U.S. and Canadian market. The mill was located in two of the present red brick buildings that were converted to a cabinet shop in 1934 and currently make up part of the Amana Furniture Shop. The smokestack was removed June 21, 1934, and the bricks were used for the building that was to become the Homestead Sandwich Shop.

Bolts of natural cotton fabric were purchased from mills in the South, then shipped to Homestead by rail and on to Amana by oxen. The dyed and finished textile (muslin) became known from coast to coast as "blue print" or "Amana calico." The dark (black and dark blue) fabrics were produced for the Amana market, while the fabrics sold to outsiders through Amana salesmen and sample books were colorful and had more intricate designs.[2] Production ranged from four hundred to four thousand yards a day. Since the dyes used to make the printed calico came from Germany, the operation was terminated with the American entry into World War I. (See Appendix A.)

Another major industrial operation was woolen mills,

27

one in Middle Amana and one in Amana. The mill in Middle Amana burned and was rebuilt about 1892; the one in Amana had a major fire in 1923 and was replaced later. Each of these mills consisted of twenty buildings and housed the finest machinery available for manufacturing woolen fabric of excellent quality.[3] Over 150,000 pounds of wool were used annually in the production of piece goods.

The mills were powered by water and steam. Even though the Iowa River was a good source of power, it was decided by the Elders in 1862 that an additional water resource would be beneficial for industrial development as well as for the livestock.[4] A strip of land seven miles long, west of the village of Amana and toward Middle Amana, was surveyed for a canal or millrace that would divert water from the Iowa River near South Amana. As the plans and project developed, teams of oxen with scrapers and crews of men with hand shovels started to excavate the forty-foot-wide waterway. A large steam-powered boat with a crane (the first of three) and large enough to house four men was built for dredging the marshy areas and clearing the silt.

Middle Amana woolen mill, 1910. The smokestack was built in 1888. It has been retained by Amana Refrigeration, Inc., which is now located on this site. The smokestack also appears in photos on pages 137 and 186. (Photographic Collection, Amana Refrigeration, Inc.)

The bridges over the waterways were constructed so that they could be removed as the dredge went up and down once each summer. The total project was completed in four years and was a tremendous engineering feat for the Inspirationists, who were untrained and inexperienced in such undertakings. It also proved to be a valuable source of water power for Amana and Middle Amana, as well as a popular swimming hole and favorite fishing spot.

Midway between Amana and Middle Amana the millrace spread out over lower lands and formed a picturesque lake that soon became edged with willows here and there. In her explanation of the creation of the lake, locally known as the "Lily Pond" or the "Pond," Elizabeth Schoenfelder wrote that a "small connecting ditch from the seven mile millrace to the swamp area created the pond as a natural reservoir for surplus water in the 1860's."[5] The lake covers about 175 acres, and in late July and early August of each year the periphery of the lake is softened by the radially symmetric pale yellow petals and dark green waxy leaves of the lotus lilies.[6]

The village of East Amana was predominantly an agricultural community with large barns and related facilities. East Amana was located on the Chicago, Milwaukee, St. Paul, and Pacific Railroad; it was a "flag stop," not a scheduled stopping point. The railroad was used primarily for shipping livestock.

Middle Amana, as the name implies, was in a central location and was the home of 380 Inspirationists. Today it is the site of Amana Refrigeration, Inc., a major manufacturer and worldwide distributor of Amana brand refrigerators, freezers, microwave ovens, and other household appliances.

High Amana and West Amana were small villages. Each had many of the same essentially self-sufficient enterprises. The early plans for High Amana were to build the village on a hill. Two houses had been erected and oxen were pulling additional lumber up the hill when a load was accidentally tipped and the wood rolled back down the incline. The Elders immediately felt that this was not a practical building site and decided the settlement should be built below the hill. Thus the complete name of the village was

Amana vor der Höhe, or "Amana in front of the hill."[7] West
Amana was located directly west of High Amana.

The Chicago, Milwaukee, St. Paul, and Pacific Railroad
was a source of much activity in South Amana, located in
the southwest corner of Amana township. Grain and livestock were shipped from this point. The railroad had a de-
pot there, and the Society built a two-story hotel nearby to
house occasional travelers.

The primary rail center for the Inspirationists was at
Homestead, the town purchased expressly for this purpose.
In addition, Homestead had a distribution warehouse. The
population was approximately 150, many of whom were
not Inspirationists. The inhabitants included individuals
who were working with the railroad at the time of the
town's purchase, as well as outsiders who were employed
by the Society to supplement the Amana work force. The
federal census of 1860 lists a relatively large number of cabinetmakers and carpenters with German and Swiss backgrounds, and it gives Homestead as the post office address
of Christian Metz.

Amana Houses and Other Structures

The architectural style of the buildings erected and
owned collectively by the Society was symbolic of the religious philosophy of those who lived, worked, and wor-
shipped in them. The exteriors as well as the interiors of the
houses, schools, meetinghouses, business enterprises,
barns, and outbuildings all expressed a visual oneness in
their simplicity of line, color, form, and purpose. With the
exception of the barns, all were essentially the same. The
structures were built in a sturdy fashion, following German
tradition, but did not possess any of the ornamentation that
might have been found on the homes of Hesse. One architectural authority pointed out the similarity of the wood
framing of the Amana buildings with that of the Gothic period.[8]

EXTERIORS. In the early years the large residential
communal houses were two stories high and symmetrical,

Frame house and sandstone house. Exteriors of buildings were of wood, brick, or sandstone. (Photographic Collection, State Historical Society of Iowa)

had a central front and central rear entrance and hallway, and usually contained eight or ten rooms. Many of the later asymmetric houses were one and one-half stories high and had six rooms; they deviated from the usual pattern by incorporating a side entrance and hall and had various other small additions, such as a washhouse. All had full basements with stone foundations up to three feet thick, exposed sills, and dirt floors. The high, gabled roofs created large spaces in the attics that were ideal for storing trunks that had been used to move personal belongings across the Atlantic to Ebenezer and then to Iowa. Other buildings of the community were similar in appearance, with usage largely determining their size.

Much of the mortised, tenoned, and pinned timber framing, joists, studding, sills, plates, rafters, sheathing, and roof boards were of solid oak and walnut. A good portion of the heavy framing timbers was hand-hewn, even though sawmills were available. The reason may have been that early sawmills were too short for the framing timbers or that the blades may not have been heavy enough for the large timbers. Also, the experienced woodsman could hand-hew a log in less time and effort than it would have taken to haul the log to and from the sawmill. Some of the ten-inch by ten-inch sills in the buildings still retain the bark on one side; the inside walls were built of eight-inch by eight-inch frames. Robert Clark wrote that "the colonists insulated the wooden houses with nogging between the studs."[9]

When the first Inspirationists migrated to Iowa they brought lumber and rope with them from the Canadian villages of Canada Ebenezer and Kenneberg so that housing could be started as soon as possible. Ruth Snyder wrote that the lumber was "shipped by boat from Buffalo to Chicago and by rail to Muscatine, Iowa, where it was hauled by ox-cart to the Amana lands. Until saw mills were built and in operation they continued to ship all their lumber for building from Ebenezer. When the Rock Island railway was extended to Davenport, Iowa, it shortened the distance for the ox-cart hauling."[10] As soon as a sawmill was built in a village, home building gained momentum, and the population began to increase. Simultaneously, the stores, workshops, mills, and barns also took form. The years between 1855 and 1865 were highly productive.

Many of the early buildings were frame, since wood was plentiful. The unpainted exterior siding of narrow pine boards exposed to the elements took on a gray, weathered look that contrasted with the background of rolling green hills and prairie grasses. In Ebenezer it had been the practice of the Inspirationists to paint the exteriors of the buildings white. In Amana it was generally assumed to be more economical to replace a building than to paint it or to insure it.

Other materials used for the exteriors were sandstone and brick. Two quarries, one near the village of Amana and the second immediately west of West Amana, provided stone as a building material. Stone was moved to the building sites on sledges pulled by teams of oxen. The sandstone from the Amana quarry was lighter in color and softer than the sandstone found near the West Amana quarry. A soft type of mortar made of local lime was the bonding material; it allowed for expansion and contraction of the building blocks. This kind of mortar has minimized cracking and spalling over the years. Most of the sandstone structures can be found in Amana and West Amana, areas near the stone sources.

Red brick buildings dominated in Middle Amana and Homestead; homes, meetinghouses, schools, stores, hotels, the woolen mill, and small business enterprises were built of brick. A good quality clay was discovered near the village of Amana, where a kiln was built; a second kiln was erected at Homestead. The bricks helped to meet the early need for building material, since the bricks were easily made at a low cost. (No bricks are produced in Amana today.) The

Original door latch made by an Amana locksmith. Many of these original door latches are still used in Amana homes and businesses. (Courtesy, Zuber's Restaurant)

frame, stone, and brick structures were topped with simple cornices and roofs of wooden shingles.

Equidistant, symmetrically placed windows and doors added welcome interest to the otherwise plain, uninterrupted facades of the look-alike buildings bordering the village roadways. The front entrances were without protective hoods or porches and had doors of panel construction headed with glazed transoms. A simple wooden handrail on one or both sides of the two or three front steps was made of boards and supported by four-sided posts. The skilled German locksmiths crafted unique square metal door latches with pull-up handles on the top; the lower section housed the base for the keyhole and ever-present key. Interior and exterior doors had the same type of latch, door after door after door. Nobody knocked, they just came in by the back door. The latches are still in use in spite of decades of opening and closing.

Fenestration was unlike that found in the surrounding Iowa countryside. The top sections of the double-hung windows were stationary and contained nine panes or "lites," while the lower sashes were movable and held six window panes. The style of smaller windows in the gabled ends was similar, with six panes in the top portion and three panes in the lower portion. The windows in the stone and brick homes were headed with segmental arches; those in the frame buildings had lintels.

Scattered here and there among the sturdy German-inspired buildings are a few homes bearing date stones in the gables, with the year of construction and, on occasion, the initials of the builder.

INTERIORS OF THE HOMES. The typical house plan provided for first- or second-floor two-room apartments for husbands and wives. Each couple had a light and airy sitting or living room and a bedroom. As the family grew, the amount of space available to them was extended. Often members of the same family, including single adults, occupied the various apartments within a single residence. Since most meals were prepared and eaten in communal kitchens, kitchens and dining rooms within the homes were not essential.[11]

A long central hall leading from the front door to the back and a traditional straight-run staircase with one hand-rail (typical in both the symmetrical and asymmetrical houses) separated some of the clusters of rooms. One closet in the front hallway under the stairway was intended for storing brooms and cleaning equipment, lamps, fuel for lamps, and candles. There were no interior closets within the apartments for the storage of clothing, a form of architectural design that was consistent with the floor plans of the homes in Europe in the 1800s as well as on the neighboring Iowa frontier. Amana *Schränke,* which were made of pine and walnut and constructed so that they could be easily disassembled for moving, were used to hold clothing.

In the early days the floors were laid with six-inch-wide white pine boards, which were scrubbed regularly with soap and water. As time passed the boards were painted or covered with colorful strips of woven rag carpeting made from scraps of leftover and unused fabric. In later years the strips of rag carpeting, thirty to thirty-two or thirty-five to thirty-six inches wide, were sewn together and covered all the floor area. A regular and thorough spring and fall house-cleaning required the removal of many black-headed, long shank tacks so the carpet could be lifted and hung outdoors on the clothesline.

The plastered walls and ceilings of the square or rectangular rooms were whitewashed in "colony blue" calcimine (a solution containing zinc oxide, water, glue, and blue coloring material). Joists and beams in the ceilings of the upstairs rooms were often exposed. The sharp-edged lines of the unframed window openings with twelve-inch reveals were softened with short curtains of white calico held in place by means of metal clips. Interior doors were of panel construction; the transoms above had five vertical rectangular panes that allowed the passage of daylight.

Fireplaces and central heating were nonexistent. Every room had a stovepipe that entered the room at the corner to accommodate the cast-iron, locally purchased, wood-burning "Wild Rose" heating stove. The stoves had trademarks indicating they had been made by Root and Jewett of Buffalo, New York. Inside chimneys for adjacent apartments were built in a common wall to minimize labor, materials,

and fuel. Two cords of wood per room per house were provided to meet the heating needs.[12] The smoke from the
wood fires in the stoves exited through chimneys that in the
early years were rectangular in shape and later were rectangular but with "bulbous tops."

*The wood-burning "Wild Rose" home heating stove of cast iron.
(Courtesy, Zuber's Restaurant)*

MEETINGHOUSES. The village meetinghouses served the most vital function for all members of the Community of True Inspiration: religious worship eleven times a week. The buildings were of the same unpretentious architectural design; their size and purpose reflected their importance. The components were similar to those of the houses; the foundations, roofs, cornices, joists, floors, and exterior details were all the same. Churches and most schools were built of stone or brick, not wood. The windows were of the same general style, but the panes were slightly larger—all in proper perspective. There were two entrances, one for men and one for women.

The interiors had the traditional blue whitewash walls, flooring of wide planks, and no altars or wall ornamentation. The men sat on one side of the center aisle, and the

Original brick meetinghouse in Homestead. Services are still held on a regular basis. Note the two separate entrances on the front, one for women and one for men.

Doorway of Homestead meetinghouse. The window on the right is typical of Amana fenestration. The top portion is a fixed window with a greater number of "lites" than the movable lower section.

women—in their black dresses, shawls, and caps—on the other, each group on pine benches that have been scrubbed semiannually through the years and now possess a unique and beautiful whitish patina. The original benches are still in use.

The buildings usually contained one large room and several smaller ones, as well as apartments at one end that were occupied by church Elders. In the village of Amana, however, the meeting room or church proper was divided into three sections by means of two removable paneled walls. These two temporary walls, made of sections of wood

Original church furniture. Many of the church benches were transported from Germany to Ebenezer and reassembled with pegs, a process repeated in the move to Amana.

two feet wide, provided the separate inner entrances for men and women, added warmth to the central section in winter, and could be conveniently converted into communion tables when needed. Cellars in most of the meetinghouses were used for the storage of wine.

Christian Metz supervised the building of most of the meetinghouses, laid the floor in the church in South Amana, and planed the entire floor of the church in High Amana.

SCHOOLS. The centrally located schools were similar to the other structures of the villages, but like the churches, they were longer and larger. The first floor of the school building was used for classes. An apartment for the schoolmaster, who was an Inspirationist and had a lifelong

This building in High Amana served as a Kinderschule *in the early days. (Photographic Collection, Amana Heritage Society)*

dedication to his profession, was on the second floor or at one end of the building. An orchard and gardens were strategically planted near the school, as the young needed exposure to the proper care of fruit trees and plants. In addition to the regular day school, each village had a *Kinderschule* for the preschool children. The building for these young children was small. Again, well-scrubbed benches and sanded floors could be found inside. The same look of plainness dominated their environment as dominated that of their older brothers and sisters.

[OPPOSITE] *A second side of the former* Kinderschule *in High Amana. The building has been upgraded and today is used as the home of the Amana Artists Guild. (Photographic Collection, Amana Heritage Society)*

COMMUNITY KITCHENS. The community kitchens were similar to the residential structures but had some identifying characteristics. One was that the simple wooden fence in front had four rather than the usual three horizontal boards. The fences separated the yard from the sidewalks and roadways and kept the cattle away from the kitchens while they were being herded through the villages on the way to the milking barns. A nearby platform accommodated the frequent deliveries of foodstuffs from the bakery, slaughterhouse, dairy, and icehouse. Small adjacent buildings, such as chicken houses and sheds for storing garden tools used for cultivating vegetables, served the needs of the kitchen workers.

The kitchens were located in a basement area or, more often, in an extension or "L" enlargement to an otherwise traditional building. The structures had long, covered side porches that served as entries to the preparation and eating areas. Between meals the kitchen supervisor and her staff could be seen sitting outside peeling potatoes or snapping green beans. The porches also served as a gathering spot for members who, while waiting for the early arrivals to finish eating, had a place to carry on a friendly exchange of ideas and other pleasantries.

The areas where the women prepared the food were large, airy, orderly, immaculate, and well supplied with conveniences of all sorts for paring, slicing, chopping, pitting, and grinding. Along one side of the room was a low wood- or charcoal-burning stove or hearth made of brick, with an iron eight-kettle hole plate to hold the cooking utensils. The stove also had a purchased bake oven and a purchased warming oven. On the wall in back of the stove was a sheet of mirrorlike tin against which were hung the kettles, pots, and pans. The cooking area was supplied with running water and a wooden trough that was used as a sink. Extra supplies of food were stored in appropriate bins in the large basements.

BARNS AND OUTBUILDINGS. Since the Inspirationists were greatly dependent on agriculture, many outbuildings were necessary to store grain and to shelter the livestock and farm equipment. Numerous barns and related structures were clustered at one end of the village—a continuation of the line of weathered facades bordering both sides of the dirt roads. The barns were of massive proportions.

The large frame barns with stone foundations were built into a hillside if the terrain permitted; they had large mows for storing hay and drying logs to be used later by the cabinetmaker. In some instances the stone wall of the foundation was extended and provided the cattle, horses, and oxen protection from inclement weather. Lean-to sheds were added wherever and whenever they were needed. The pigs had the advantage of being housed in piggeries built only for them.

Outbuildings adjacent to or sometimes attached to the residences included woodsheds and drying houses for vegetables. The outdoor toilet could be found along the walking path at the back, within a short distance of the communal residential houses. As is frequent today, they were unisex; however, that word was unlikely to have been in the vocabulary of the colonists in 1865.

Each village had a washhouse where the clothing of outside hired workers was washed by women assigned to that task. Washhouses had large open hearths similar to those in the communal kitchens for heating the water that had to be carried from the cisterns. The large kettles rested on the edge of round openings of the flat surface of the stove and were heated by corn cob and wood fires underneath.

The wood that served as fuel for the washhouses, communal kitchens, homes, and other heated buildings was logged by crews of men, transported by teams of oxen or horses, cut into lengths appropriate for the heating stoves, and rolled into the yards. Occasionally the head of a household would independently harness a team and gather wood to supplement his allotment. He and other members of his extended family would fasten chains to three or four logs, and the animals would pull the logs on a sleigh or wagon to the village sawmill. It was the responsibility of the young boys to move the cut lengths from the front yards to the woodsheds in the back. The logs would be stacked neatly and with great precision.

After the ashes from wood fires in the various buildings were cooled, they were deposited in a small village ash house.[13] Later they were transferred to the two-room soap house, where two large vats half buried in the floor were used for making bulk and bar soap.

Wine was made in small frame and unpainted buildings called press houses, which usually were located near the churches.

CHAPTER 4

The Amana Society, 1855–1932

Amana-style Communal Living

A communal system developed gradually as the members of the Community of True Inspiration moved from Hesse to Ebenezer to Amana. It provided a means of living together as efficiently as possible, while allowing members maximum time for religious worship. The system did not evolve as a social theory; it grew out of necessity and circumstance. It held the group together and apart from the influence of the outside world, and it extended to all phases of life.

The constitution of the Community of True Inspiration in Iowa, known as the Amana Society, was similar to the one in Ebenezer; it became effective on January 1, 1860. All members of lawful age, male and female, signed the constitution, thereby indicating their acceptance of its provisions.

The constitution gave emphasis to the idea that the motives of the Society were religious and not worldly or selfish. Provision was made for the common ownership of land and capital. The income from land and industrial enterprises was to be used to defray the expenses of the Society. Any surplus was to be used for improvements, education, health, and the general welfare.

Membership was varied. People had come from a diversity of European backgrounds, wealth, and professions. Members were duty bound to give their property to the common fund, for which credit was given in the books of the Society and a receipt secured by the Society common property. The amounts contributed ranged from little or nothing to as much as fifty thousand dollars.[1] Individuals could retain or own household furnishings, personal possessions, and small tools. All were required to give up claims for wages, interest, and profits. In return, income and care were provided for old age, sickness, and infirmity. Provisions were made for the care of orphans and the transfer and disposition of credits or debts of deceased members to their heirs or, if there were none, to the Society. Members who left the Society by their own choice or by expulsion were entitled to receive back money they had paid into the common fund, with the amount of interest to be determined by the board of trustees but not to exceed five percent. A schedule of repayment of these and other entitlements, such as inheritances, was established for each case so as not to create undue financial difficulties for the Society.

New members were periodically added from outside the Society. Most of them came from Germany; a sizable number were friends or relatives of existing members. Those who sought to become members were carefully scrutinized to determine the sincerity of their religious beliefs and their motives for seeking membership. There was a two-year probation period during which prospective members were expected to follow Society rules, to work diligently, and to demand no wages. Those who were accepted had to turn over their property to the Society and sign the constitution. A few people were accepted without probation. In addition, the Society employed a number of nonmember hired hands, almost all Germans.

Housing was provided without cost to families and unmarried individuals. The houses were occupied by more than one family unit; an effort was made to adapt to individual preferences and give privacy. When possible, residents were housed close to their work assignments. There were no kitchens or dining rooms in the homes. Each family did its own washing in a washhouse attached to the residence.

Nonmembers who were needed for the extra labor lived

in separate housing that was especially built for them at the edges of the villages. The nonmembers who worked in the timberlands were housed in small "shanties" in the wooded areas, away from the villages where the workers would stay during the week. The communal kitchens provided them with a supply of bread, meat, cheese, molasses, and other foodstuffs to meet their needs for several days. *Landstreicheren*, or "migrants," commonly known as hoboes and tramps, would stop at the Amana villages periodically as they traveled across the country on the nearby railroads. They would be asked to do work such as cleaning chicken houses and outdoor toilets or other handyman duties in exchange for food and housing. As many as ten or twelve would be waiting at a communal kitchen in the mornings after the members of the Society had finished eating. The shelter provided was usually a lean-to attached to the community washhouse. Some would be asked to stay a few days; others would be encouraged to stay a few years.

The people ate in common kitchen houses, which were conveniently located. The structures varied in number with the size of the village; Amana had a maximum of sixteen kitchens, and each would accommodate forty or fifty people. Men and women ate at separate tables. Single male adults ate at the hotel, because single young females helped in the kitchens with food preparation. For people who were ill or for women who cared for young children, food was carried in baskets to the homes. Even the night watchman would have a midnight lunch prepared and set out for him. Breakfast was normally served from 6:00 to 6:30 A.M., dinner at 11:30 A.M., and supper from 6:00 to 7:00 P.M. During the winter months an afternoon lunch was served, and in the summer a midmorning and midafternoon lunch was available. Beer or wine was sometimes added.

The meat for the kitchens came from the butcher shops, flour from the village mill, and milk and cheese from the dairy. There were large gardens for growing vegetables, orchards for fruit, and henneries for eggs. Staple grocery items were provided by the village stores.

The work pattern of the community kitchen was a prime example of cooperative endeavor. Each kitchen was under the direction of a kitchen supervisor who was ap-

Zimmerman communal kitchen. Today it is the Ronneburg Restaurant. (Photographic Collection, State Historical Society of Iowa)

pointed to her position by the Elders, and her kitchen informally assumed her last name; Mrs. Zimmerman's kitchen became known as the Zimmerman kitchen, Mrs. Dickel's kitchen was called the Dickel kitchen, and so on.

The young women who worked under the kitchen supervisor alternated the various tasks necessary in the preparation and serving of food five times a day. It was not unusual to see several young women sitting outdoors on long benches, holding large, traylike cutting boards while preparing an abundance of vegetables for the next meal. Others were busily preparing a midmorning lunch or perhaps making unsalted butter or cheese. Only the products of the village bakery, meat market, and dairy were delivered once or twice a day; most of the other food was prepared by the women. The kitchens were slightly competitive, as each staff was eager to maintain a reputation for delicious meals, just as each young lady was pleased to be credited with the honor of making the best doughnuts or cakes. The system freed those women not engaged in the preparation of food for other kinds of productive work for the Society. The Elders assigned one man to each kitchen to help the women with any heavy or unpleasant tasks.

The entire kitchen operation was executed according to plan. During the summer the Monday menu was the same week after week; Wednesday night supper during the winter months varied little, and so on. Pork, the favored meat, was converted into many kinds of wursts, roasts, bacon, and ham, while beef was frequently boiled, roasted, or ground for patties. Thanksgiving and Christmas were days for serving chicken.

It was the responsibility of the kitchen staff to take care of the vegetable gardens and to harvest fresh fruits and vegetables as the season progressed. Yellow Ebenezer onions, which were cultivated by these women from seeds brought from Hesse, were especially palatable. The choice onions were kept for seed, seconds were sold in market areas as far away as Chicago, and the standards flavored Amana soups and stews. The children often helped with the sorting. Garden produce included salsify, root celery (celeriac), and ground cherries—all items that are uncommon in Iowa today. Many vegetables were preserved for use during the winter months; kale was dried, carrots and other root vegetables were stored in boxes of sand in the cellars, beans were salted down to be prepared later with ham and onions, and large quantities of cabbage were cut for sauerkraut. The late summer was an especially busy time, with canning and making pickles and preserves.

The food was well prepared, plentiful, and nutritious. Table talk was generally discouraged during the time the members gathered together on the unpainted backless benches at the long, narrow, oilcloth-covered tables, yet the feelings of *Gemeinschaft* (community) and brotherhood that existed at mealtime served as an additional unifying force within a community unto itself. The Elders would sit together at one end of the table.

Each village had a separate agricultural unit supervised by a farm manager, who would assign tasks to those who could do them best. Certain individuals were responsible for the horses, oxen, sheep, hogs, and dairy and beef cattle housed in the barns and sheds at the edge of the village. Some livestock were sold to an outside market, while others were slaughtered and cured, pickled, or smoked. The dairies provided the milk and the cream. A relatively small amount of poultry was raised.

The coopershops made kegs, churns, tubs, buckets, and barrels for beer, wine, cider, oil, grease, and brine. The men of the wagon shops were responsible for sleighs, wagons, wheelbarrows, and implements. The wagon wheels were made of wood that was first steamed and then curved into shape.

The village stores served as the distribution point for other needs. Except for trade with outsiders, no money was used. Each adult male was given an annual allowance of forty to one hundred dollars depending on his need for clothing and other necessities. A physician might be given the top amount because his style of life had special requirements. A person whose occupation required frequent re-

West Amana general store. This store and the store in Amana were popular shopping stops for nearby farmers who delivered grain to the mills in the villages to be ground for flour.

placements of clothing might be given a higher amount. Women were given from twenty-five to thirty dollars, and for each child there was five to ten dollars. The members carried account books to record the credits and debits that resulted from purchases at the general store. The prices charged by the store for items such as clothing, hats or caps, shoes, dry goods, drugs, watches, tobacco, and candy were determined by the cost of these items plus the expense of distribution. Entries were made with each purchase, and the amounts not used could be saved for the next year. The stores carried only the necessities of a simple life-style; for example, earrings for young women were not available. Credits could also be exchanged for the services of craftsmen. A man might buy fabric for a suit and take it to the tailor, who would charge a specified amount.

While every effort was made to be self-sufficient, some items were obtained from the outside. Requests from all the villages were received by the office of the Amana Society, and the transactions were handled through that office. The cabinetmaker, for example, would need ingredients for the homemade varnish for furniture, sheets of glue, and upholstery fabric. The general stores in Homestead and South Amana purchased and sold to members some pieces of furniture, such as pine chairs, particularly at times when the demands of the members could not be supplied fast enough by Society craftsmen.

An elaborate system of accounting was maintained. In addition to the bookkeeping transactions for the village stores and consumer services, the system was used for the business enterprises. For example, the carpenter or the blacksmith shop would charge the farm department, which in turn would receive credits for agricultural products. Each village did much of its own record keeping, but the accounts were consolidated at Amana Society headquarters. The capital and operating budgets, as well as the balance sheets and operating statements, were maintained there.

At the end of the year, some villages might experience a net loss and others a profit. For example, a farming village might have a bad crop during one growing season, while Amana, with its intensive manufacturing, might have a large profit. Changing economic conditions would vary the relative profits and losses for the different villages and economic enterprises. Whatever the outcome for a village, the shelter, food, and allowances for families and individuals would be the same throughout the Society. This aspect of Amana communal living was something like that envisioned by communist idealism. Metz organized and directed the development of a communal plan so that all members would participate in the work and all would reap the rewards.

Governance of the Society

The constitution provided for the governance of the Society and for the conduct of Society business enterprises. A board of trustees consisting of thirteen members was annually elected from the roster of Elders by members of the Society entitled to vote. Those eligible to vote included male members who had signed the constitution, and widows and female members over thirty years of age not represented by a male member. Three of the trustees came from the largest village and Society headquarters, Amana; two from each of four villages; and one from each of the two smallest villages.

This board was the top governing body of the Society and was the high court of appeal for all disputes and complaints. These trustees were simultaneously the Great Council of Elders, which was the governing authority on all spiritual affairs. When the *Werkzeuge* Christian Metz and Barbara Heinemann were still living, the council would consult with them prior to making a decision. After their deaths the council was the supreme religious authority.

The trustees elected a president, vice president, and secretary from among their own numbers on the second Tuesday of December for a term of one year. As Bertha Shambaugh pointed out, "The incumbents are usually reelected; for rotation in office has never been a part of the Amana theory of government."[2] It has been noted by some members of the Society that the board succeeded itself by renominating its own members, and if succession became necessary due to disability or death they generally nominated new members along family lines. This practice provided a large measure of continuity and stability in policy, but it also weakened the general esprit de corps. Critics have called this system of government "an aristocracy of Elders," producing too much distinction between the governing and the governed.[3] On the other hand, historical graveyards are filled with communal and religious societies who failed for lack of effective governance.

The powers vested in the trustees were comprehensive and considerable, including the rights to admit new members, assign work, fix allowances, and discipline members. In addition there were responsibilities relating to accounting, finance and investment, contracts and legal matters, agriculture and manufacturing, and other aspects of the business side of the Amana Society. In matters of great importance and responsibility the trustees were required by the constitution to hold special meetings to determine whether a vote by the Elders or Society members would be necessary to resolve a problem.

Each village was governed by its own board of Elders, the number ranging from eighteen in the largest village to seven in the smallest. This board, called the *Bruderrat,* included the resident trustee, who was considered to be the highest authority on temporal matters. The head Elder of the village was the highest authority on religious matters, even though the trustee was a member of the Great Council.[4] The leading village Elders appointed foremen and determined the duties assigned to individuals. Personal preferences were considered but were not always controlling. Furthermore, work assignments changed with overall needs. For example, the cabinetmakers, locksmiths, and other craftsmen, as well as women, might be assigned to work in the fields during harvest. Adjustments in the labor supply were made to clean the millrace annually, repair flood damage, clear the roads of snow when necessary, and harvest the yearly supply of ice. All males who were physically able were members of the fire department. Some aspects of Amana governance were determined by the governmental structure of the state of Iowa.

Except for a small area in Johnson County, Amana land was located in Iowa County, primarily in Lenox Township, with small plots in Iowa, Hilton, Marengo, and Washington townships. In 1854 Lenox Township was divided into two townships, Amana and Lenox.⁵ The first election of Amana township officers was held in the Amana schoolhouse. The township trustees, the justices, the clerk, and the assessor were all members of the Amana Society. Legal matters were handled at Marengo, the county seat of Iowa County, and in Des Moines, the capital. Outside lawyers were employed, since Amana had no lawyers among its members.

Religion and Religious Observances

Religion was the unifying force among the members of the Community of True Inspiration. It was the basis for economic, social, and educational activity. It was the bond that held the members together in true fellowship through many years of trial and tribulation.

The primary purpose for the existence of the Amana Society was to have freedom of worship. The Inspirationists believed in the Bible and fashioned their lives according to the teachings of Christ and the Apostles. Their lives were lived in prayer and worship, and they believed in divine inspiration and revelation. They had a firm belief in the power of the *Werkzeuge* to bring them messages directly from God. All testimonies of the *Werkzeuge* were recorded, respected, and revered. Many have been printed and bound; the revelations became the sermons of the church.⁶ Three documents also helped form the religious foundation: *The Twenty-one Rules for the Examination of Our Daily Lives, The Twenty-four Rules for True Godliness,* and *Der Glauben,* which is similar to the Apostles' Creed. (See Appendix B.)

CHURCH SERVICES. Members attended regular services eleven times a week and special services on religious holidays. The services were conducted in German, and all members were expected to attend. The customary devotional consisted of a silent prayer, chanted hymn, Bible lesson, sermon or reading, comments by the Elders and/or any of the group attending, another hymn, and another prayer.

There was no instrumental accompaniment; a song leader directed the singing of hymns.

The men and women, with hymn book and Bible in hand, waited together in front of the meetinghouse until all had assembled, then reverently entered at the same time

Pegged wooden clothes rack found in meetinghouses. The clothing items are typical outerwear of early Amana residents. The chair is a Barbara Heinemann chair; its seat is lower than usual because it was made especially for her to accommodate her short stature. (Courtesy, Amana Heritage Society)

but through separate doorways. The men sat on one side, the women on the other; the children in front, the adults in back. Separation of the sexes helped discourage any opportunity for flirtatious glances. The Elders, the religious leaders of the Society, had no pulpit but sat behind a simple straight-legged table in the front, facing the members. In the early days a white cloth was used as a table covering. Later this was replaced with a dark green baize, a woolen or

[OPPOSITE] *A table used by the presiding Elder in front of the church. (Courtesy, Amana Heritage Society)*

cotton fabric napped to imitate felt, which had been used in Europe for game tables in the 1700s.

The dimly lit room was austere but comfortably warm—nothing to distract from the Word of God. The walls were whitewashed Amana blue and unadorned, woven rag carpet strips often delineated the aisles, and the frequently scrubbed plain benches were arranged in straight rows from front to back and side to side. The women and young ladies wore their best ankle-length black calico or wool dresses, which had short bodices and wide waistbands. The full skirts were topped with aprons and the waists with triangular shawls, so as to cover much of the profile of the torso. Small black lace caps were worn over the center-parted, pulled-back, severe coiffures. The bearded men (no mustaches were allowed) wore black Amana-tailored suits and brimmed hats. After the service the men and women departed through the same separate doorways they had entered. On occasion, an Inspirationist might behave in some manner that met with the disapproval of the Elders; the punishment would be prohibiting the individual from attending services for a specified period of time.

Out of tradition and respect for their church, Amana women of today continue the practice of wearing small black lace caps, aprons, and dark shawls. Some of the apparel has been handed down from a mother or grandmother. Men wear dark suits and ties.

SPECIAL OBSERVANCES. The most important religious observance was that of communion, otherwise known as *Liebesmahl*, or "Lovefeast." Charles Nordhoff wrote that "it is held only when the 'inspired instrument' directs it, which may not happen once in two years; and it is thought so solemn and important an occasion that a full account of it is sometimes printed in a book."[7] He further relates that considerable time and effort were given to the many aspects of physical, psychological, and religious preparation for the event. This was a time of self-renewal and self-examination. At times the members who were considered the most devout or of the highest order participated in special rituals of the *Liebesmahl*, such as foot washing, which was considered an act of humility in the time of Jesus. After several days the observance culminated in the serving of bread and wine, which was passed along to the members by the Elders. The service was concluded with a simple meal.

Confession was held annually. Shambaugh describes one aspect of the system used by the Elders and *Werkzeuge* for the annual review of the depth of religious belief and dedication of the individual members. The Inspirationists were divided into three levels or orders (*Versammlungen*): First *Versammlungen*, Second or Middle *Versammlungen*, and *Kinder Versammlungen*, according to age and degree of religious maturity. Acting improperly, getting married, or giving birth could alter one's status and be evident by the assignment of a less desirable seating assignment in the meetinghouse.[8] There were no baptismal services; the Inspirationists believed that baptism was a spiritual rather than a physical exercise.

The traditional religious holidays of Christmas and Easter were celebrated in a serious and simple fashion. Christmas was a three-day period of worship and feasting; the children received gifts that were small and often practical. A young woman told of getting a walnut rocker for her sixteenth birthday. She said, "I wanted a bicycle, but in these days (1916) girls weren't supposed to ride bicycles."[9]

The wedding ceremony was a simple service that was usually held in the meetinghouse, often on Thursday. In early years the young woman would be asked to provide the Elders with the names of those individuals she would like to invite. Since the occasion was not to attract great attention, the Elders might choose to eliminate the names of the more distant relatives and friends so as to limit the size of the wedding to twenty-five or thirty guests. The service consisted of a hymn, prayer, Scripture and sermon, and additional prayer shared with the assembled group of relatives and friends. No rings, no flowers, no nuptial music. The bride wore her best dress (black) and the groom his best suit (black).[10] After the service congratulations were extended to the bride and groom, and the entire group moved to a communal kitchen where light German-style refreshments were served. The young couple then visited the homes of each of their parents, the groom's home first.[11]

Many of the early religious groups viewed marriage

People walking home after church services in Amana. (Photographic Collection, Amana Heritage Society)

with varying degrees of reservation. The Inspirationists considered the celibate state as being more godly than the state of marriage. In *The Twenty-one Rules for the Examination of Our Daily Lives,* a document written in 1715 for the Pietists (Inspirationists) by Eberhard Gruber to set forth a code for daily conduct, rule 20 states: "Dinners, weddings, feasts, avoid entirely; at best there is sin."

In the years that followed, a somewhat more liberal interpretation was developed. A betrothed young man and his fiancée would be required to be separated, usually for a period of one year, with each living in a different village. During the westward move to Iowa, one might have been in Ebenezer and the other in Amana. If the marriage was still foremost in their minds after the twelve-month period of being apart and the young couple received the approval of the Elders on both moral and religious grounds, permission for marriage would be granted. The wedding date would be set for a year ahead. DuVal stated that the wedding partners also had to stay apart for two weeks following the ceremony.[12]

Marriage resulted in a lowering of status of the individuals; they were assigned less desirable seating space in the church services. Gradually status was regained, but it was again lost with the birth of a child.

Wedding gifts were practical items. One couple received a wooden bucket made at the coopershop. Another was given an ironing board made by the bride's father.

If a young woman did become pregnant during the year apart, the young man and woman had to continue to be apart for a full year, followed by another year of courtship. Then they could marry!

An unpublished personal report written by a member about another family relates an incident in the Amanas that took place in the late 1850s. Iowa City was then the westernmost point of the railroad, and freight was being moved from Iowa City to Amana by ox cart while the railway was being completed. A young woman of Amana who was a member of a fine, respected family became enamored of one member of the railroad crew working to expedite transportation to Homestead. The young man was a German immigrant, not an Inspirationist but of high birth, who had come to the United States without his family. He was intelligent, talented, and virile. She became pregnant. At the time of the birth of the child to this unmarried mother, her situation, the child, and the mother were accepted by Society members. Later she married an Inspirationist and had additional children.

ATTITUDE OF METZ CONCERNING MARRIAGE. DuVal wrote that "Metz did not actively oppose marriage even though he thought that it was closely associated with sin." He also commented that "the Inspirationists did not oppose matrimony if it were sanctified, but that an unmarried status was much better."[13] It became a Society requirement that when two people married they had to announce their intentions to the Elders and abide by the custom of staying apart for one year prior to the marriage to indicate that their intentions were valid.

DuVal further wrote that a poem was found in a walnut chest that had been handcrafted for Metz's daughter in the cabinet shop at the Armenburg Castle in Germany by Metz's assistant, Heinrich Kramar. The message of the poem was to discourage the daughter from taking marriage vows with the man she had hoped to marry. Eight years later she married in Ebenezer, but she then married the assistant cabinetmaker who had made the chest. The wedding occurred at a period of community development that Metz had described as not a time for weddings but a time for work.

LAST SERVICE IN THE LIFE OF AN INSPIRATIONIST. Death was treated as a fact of life; life is not eternal. When a member died, the clock in the household was stopped in order to make an accurate determination of the time of death. The cabinetmaker was called to measure the body so that the coffin could be built to the correct size and no materials would be wasted. The body was packed in ice and lay in an open, walnut-stained coffin in the parlor of the home.

The last piece of furniture in the life of an Inspirationist. The coffin. The Amana Furniture Shop makes the coffins for Society members. (Courtesy, Amana Furniture Shop)

It was the custom of the Inspirationists, as well as neighboring midwesterners of many religious denominations, to have relatives or close friends stay with the deceased during the day and night before the time of burial. One particular night two serious-minded, inexperienced young men were sitting with the body of a deceased relative. It was a very quiet and dark night outside, and oil lamps provided a minimum of illumination on the inside. In the early hours of the morning the spring mechanism in the pulled roller shade at the window failed to hold, and the shade suddenly and noisily popped and rolled to the top. The boys were very frightened; they left the body and the home, and ran quickly down the street—an incident about which the then young men have often been reminded.

The religious service at the meetinghouse was simple, with a prayer, Scripture or sermon, biographical sketch, and another prayer. No flowers, no instrumental music, and no outward expression of grief. After the service friends and relatives stopped at the home of the deceased to pay last respects, and all started to prepare to accompany the body to the cemetery. The lid of the coffin—a flat board—was pegged or screwed into place, and then the casket was mounted on a horse-drawn *Leichenwagen* and the brothers (in pairs) and sisters (in pairs) followed behind, with their placement in the procession determined according to their relationship to the loved one.

The cemeteries, which are located on the edge of the villages, are serene areas, with the only plants being beautiful, tall, regularly spaced evergreens. The graves are arranged in order of death, not according to individual families. In the earlier days (about 1885) wooden markers painted white with black letters and in later years white concrete markers were evenly spaced in straight rows, as if on a grid—another expression of the orderliness, discipline, and planning so characteristic of all phases of Amana life. Each marker gives only the person's name and the dates of birth and death. The earliest in Amana is dated 1856. Flowers are not placed on a grave at the time of burial but are placed there on each Memorial Day.

Several days after the funeral, personal items such as shawls and neckties were given to close relatives and friends as remembrances to be treasured. The bereaved were consoled in the belief that death is but the release of the spirit from pain, sorrow, and suffering, which is the lot of man during his pilgrimage on earth.

The body of Christian Metz was laid to rest in the cemetery west of Amana.

Education

The religious and academic education of Amana youth was considered to be an important aspect of life in the Community of True Inspiration. Each of the seven villages had its own school, and there was a school district within Amana township. Although the schools were under the jurisdiction of the Society, each was operated independently from the others, and the headmaster was allowed to use his own methods and approaches to teaching.

Village schoolroom setting. Girls sat on one side of the room and boys sat on the other side. Each had a hand-held slate for recitations. (Courtesy, Amana Heritage Society)

The headmaster had a lifelong position and had numerous parents and later their children in his classes through the years. In the larger schools the teaching staff sometimes included an additional male teacher or two, and on occasion a woman who assisted with the teaching of handiwork and the primary grades. The teachers were considered to be competent in that they had to attend a county-sponsored teacher accreditation course periodically and be evaluated by the county superintendent. Some also took additional work through a University of Chicago correspondence school program.

All children between the ages of five and fourteen attended school from early in the morning until late in the afternoon six days a week, fifty-two weeks a year. The only exceptions were church and national holidays and a period of ten days or two weeks in the fall when their help was needed for harvesting the crops. The Elders believed that the children as well as the adults needed to be kept busy at all times—no idleness.

Each of the schools had a small library of carefully chosen books. At the end of the school week the children would be allowed to take books to their respective homes for the weekend. Frequently all the family members would read the books before they were returned on Monday. Some of the reading needs were met by a circulating library.

The Society made available a few selected publications, such as the *Chicago Tribune, Successful Farming, National Geographic,* and some technical and trade journals. *Werkzeug* Barbara Heinemann was especially concerned with the exposure to worldliness in the reading of newspapers and other literature. If unapproved reading material were found, the Elders would publicly express their disapproval and prohibit its existence.

Religious regulations and principles were the foundation of the daily instruction of the children. Each day began by singing a psalm and saying a prayer while on bended knee. Catechism and biblical history were a part of the religious training. The academic curriculum included basic courses as taught in other schools in the county—U.S. history, physiology, geography, spelling, reading, writing, arithmetic, and grammar.

Amana girls enjoying their "play hour" at the Homestead school (ca. 1925). Hours for school days were from 7:00 to 11:30 A.M. and 12:30 to 6:00 P.M. (Photographic Collection, Amana Heritage Society)

As a wintertime activity at school, the six-year-old boys and girls were taught to knit. They became sufficiently skilled to knit enough gloves and mittens to meet the needs of the community and to have extras to sell to a Chicago market. The boys knit the fingers, while the girls made the body of the gloves and attached the fingers. During the summer months this activity was replaced with learning how to care for flowers, plants, and trees. Lessons were interspersed with lunches of warm rye or whole wheat bread and butter.

The girls in their black caps and long dresses sat on one side of the classroom and the boys in their bib overalls on the other. All were the proud possessors of hand-held slates, which were used in making recitations. A calendar and a copy of the twenty-six characters of the German alphabet may have been on the wall. The children were well mannered and courteous and would extend a hand for a handshake in a greeting or a good-bye. Although these young people learned German at home and used it in the lower

Two children sitting on a wagon. (Photographic Collection, Amana Heritage Society)

grades, they learned English in school; on completion of the eighth grade they took countywide competitive proficiency examinations to earn a certificate. The Elders and the teachers also conducted a long, solemn graduation ceremony for the eighth graders, during which the students were given a comprehensive questioning in both the religious and academic areas.

When the formal education of the young women was terminated at age fourteen, the Elders would assign them to work in communal kitchens. Fourteen-year-old young men would be assigned apprenticeships in occupations where they were needed. Tastes and talents as well as the preferences of parents were taken into consideration. As the need arose, a few young males were selected to continue their high school education in the nearby town of Marengo, the county seat, then to go on to the University of Iowa in medicine, dentistry, or pharmacy.

The schools of the Amana Society were public, not parochial, and thus were able to share in state funds.

CHAPTER 5

Furniture in
Early Amana Life

T he design and craftsmanship of furniture have had special places in the history of Amana. Through-out the years the Society cabinetmakers have continued to maintain their high standards and to seek a perfection and a beauty that have become their trademark.

Interior Furniture and Furnishings

As a girl approached womanhood, her thoughts quite naturally turned to the possibilities of marriage and a future home of her own. With this in mind she started accumulating, piece by piece, a number of household items, including furniture. Since marriage was not permitted until young men attained the age of twenty-four, there was often sufficient time to gain a considerable stock of furniture through inheritance, gifts, and other means. Major pieces that the bride and groom did not possess by the time of their marriage might have been given as wedding presents by friends or relatives, or if need be, could be ordered from a cabinetmaker. The style of the furniture in the home of a young Amana couple was generally simple and straight-lined and very much like that found in every other Amana home. On occasion there were pieces that were more elaborate, since they had been especially made. Small items accumulated before a marriage were stored in a plain, square, boxlike hinged chest similar to a traditional hope chest.

Furnishings were personal possessions. The furniture of the living room, or *Wohnzimmer*, would probably include a sofa, side chairs, rocker, footstool, chest-on-chest, table, hanging wall clock, and paper rack. Most families were fortunate to have at least one piece that had been brought from Germany or Ebenezer, or perhaps a piece that had been made from the small quantity of black walnut shipped from Germany to Ebenezer for the purpose of making furniture. German walnut was considered to be an especially fine and beautiful furniture wood. However, high shipping costs stopped the importation of such walnut.

The sofa, or *Bank*, a multiple seating piece, was usually made in one of two basic designs. Both had a considerable amount of plain and unadorned exposed walnut or cherry along the front apron, back rails, and arms. The seat and back were without springs but were stuffed with horsehair and upholstered in a heavy fabric of solid color.

A few sofas from early Amana still exist. One type had a wooden back with no padding or upholstery on either side. The other had padding and upholstery only on the front; the wood was fully exposed on the back. A small, round footstool with four tapered and turned legs was found in every living room. The top was upholstered in a fabric similar to that of the sofa.

Typical Amana upholstered walnut footstool. Every living room had at least one footstool, the styles of which varied considerably. Some were upholstered, others had finished wood tops. (Courtesy, Berger Custom Woodwork Shop)

Old traditional sofa. Sofas of this basic style can be seen in Amana homes. The seat and back have no springs and are stuffed with horsehair and covered with a heavy, hard-surface fabric of solid color. (Courtesy, Amana Heritage Society)

Amana sofa. This basic style reflects strong Victorian (serpentine-arched top rail) and American Empire (half-lyre-curved ends and bracket feet) influences. The rails, ends, and apron have exposed wood; the upholstery is attached with long-shank upholstery tacks. (Courtesy, Amana Heritage Society)

The design of the straight chairs varied somewhat, but often some form of a spindle back with a low, solid rail was used. The chairs had many of the characteristics of the early Windsor chairs. Old European household inventories suggest that the beechwood spindle back was developed in and around Windsor, England, about 1675, with the design

Painted pine side chair, ca. 1875. This chair from the Wagon Room at Zuber's Restaurant in Homestead is one of the original ones used at the former hotel. Note the spindle back. (Courtesy, Zuber's Restaurant)

being credited to the men whose trade was the making and repairing of wheel spokes—the wheelwrights. There is also evidence that the spindle backs may have been developed independently on the European continent. A painting produced in Germany in 1739 shows two spindle-back chairs similar to those produced in England but with more elaborate rails atop the spindles and raked legs.[1]

The design of the spindle-back chair was brought to America by immigrants from Europe. American colonists liked this chair form because it was lightweight, sturdy, easy to construct, and could be made of numerous kinds of unseasoned wood. As a seating piece, it was aesthetically pleasing and satisfied the needs of frontier living. This chair was made throughout New England and the North Atlantic states; the foremost center was Philadelphia, which was the home of many highly skilled German cabinetmakers and chair makers. Many modifications of the spindle back were in common use in homes and public places when Christian Metz and his colleagues first traveled in America to search for a new home. Metz, a cabinetmaker as well as a *Werkzeug*, was undoubtedly aware of the furniture designs he saw. The low-back side chair with spindles and solid straight rail and the spindle-back arm chair became the Ebenezer and Amana versions of this chair.

At the time the Iowa villages were being built and the homes furnished, the material needs of the Inspirationists were many. Chairs handcrafted by Amana cabinetmakers did not necessarily take precedence over commercially

[OPPOSITE] *Painted pine arm chair, ca. 1875. This chair from the Wagon Room at Zuber's Restaurant in Homestead is one of the originals used at the former hotel. The style, often referred to as a "captain's chair," reflects some influence of the Windsor-type chairs developed in the Philadelphia area during the eighteenth century with a low-shaped rail across the top of the back. The heavy arm is continuous from one side to the other. The seat is deep and U-shaped, the front legs have ring turning, the back legs are plain, and all four legs are braced with double stretchers. (Courtesy, Zuber's Restaurant)*

Walnut youth or bar chair. This chair form incorporates details found in Amana chair design of an earlier day—a spindle back, simple turning, splayed legs, and bracket support. (Courtesy, Amana Furniture Shop)

[BELOW] *Old Amana desk chair that was made to tilt and swivel. Note the detail of the carving. (Courtesy, Connie Zuber)*

made chairs if there were other priorities for the labor of the cabinetmaker. Because the construction of a chair required considerable time and inexpensive pine chairs were available from outside manufacturers, chairs were purchased by the general stores in the villages with depots (South Amana and Homestead).[2]

The cabinetmakers of the early days worked only for the betterment of the Society and not for their own individual welfare and recognition; they did not identify any of their creations with a mark, initials, or name. It is therefore sometimes difficult to identify the source of a few of the old existing chairs that have had long and hard use.

There are in Amana today a limited number of old side and arm spindle-back chairs that were painted black with a narrow yellow or red band outlining the back and seat. The black was possibly suggestive of ebony, a wood that was in popular demand in Europe about the time the Society migrated. Wagon seats were treated in much the same manner. Two adaptations of this basic chair, the captain's chair and the spindle-back settee, are currently being made by the Amana cabinetmakers.

Pieces of furniture that were sectional were not unusual. Some pedestal tables were composed of a separate base, legs, and top. More common was the chest-on-chest, which could be found in a living room or bedroom, the location determined by the size of the piece and space available. The lower portion of the massive and impressive chest-on-chest consisted of a series of four drawers with simple round wooden pulls, or of drawers plus two paneled doors. The foot was usually of a bracket type, and the keyholes were inlaid. The profile of the apron was plain or had simple carving. The top chest, usually about two-thirds the depth of the lower section, had two solid paneled doors on the front and was built with the same general simple lines of construction. If the upper half were to be used for the storage of religious books or items of irregular shape, the interior of the section was made with pegs on the sides so that the shelves would be adjustable. A harmonious, curved molding sometimes edged the top of each section.

The ends of most chests and other case pieces had recessed solid panels. The large undecorated sections with a hand-rubbed finish gave an unequaled quality of strength and quiet uniformity to these pieces. A long, narrow, neat white cloth runner edged with crocheted handiwork protected the open shelf created by the greater depth of the lower chest. In those instances where the bottom and top half were of the same depth, the top surface of the floor section was unfinished.

A commode was frequently found in the homes that did not have a chest-on-chest in the living room. This piece was about four feet high and had five drawers with round wooden pulls. The lines were similar to those of the lower part of the chest-on-chest except that a commode was taller. Again, a fresh white runner was always placed on the top surface. One such commode found in an Amana home today was made from a walnut tree that had been struck by lightning and had fallen into a stream of water. The wood looked so fine that the workmen removed it from the water and took it to the nearby cabinet shop where the cabinetmaker made a commode from it after the wood was properly aged.

A few of the chests made in Ebenezer and transported from there had a top drawer that would pull down in front to serve as a writing surface. Not many such pieces were made in Amana because labor and time were scarce.

Every home had a paper rack on the wall, even though Society members were not encouraged to read a great deal. The design of the rack varied considerably, but it had a flat backing of wood with an incised, painted, embroidered, or cutout second piece hinged at the lower edge to provide an angled pocket for holding papers. These racks were made by cabinetmakers, or in some instances by men who liked to occupy their spare time with woodworking. Other wall accessories included seed pictures, samplers, or embroidered prayers. A translation of a framed German message might read "I have found life's happiest hours within the family circle" or "God will care for you." Corner floor-standing whatnot shelves provided space for displaying a few pieces of antique glassware and family heirlooms.

During the 1800s the use of photographs and pictures as a means of lending decoration to a room was discouraged. This austerity gradually changed. However,

Chest-on-chest. A piece of fabric, such as baize, or a crisp white cloth trimmed with a crocheted edge would be placed between the upper and lower sections or on the front shelf created by the difference in depth between the two sections. The device near the center of the shelf is a Zünd Machien, or ignition machine. The turned wooden holder on the left contained paper tapers, which when ignited were inserted into the device (with blue vitriol) to create illumination for a room. (Courtesy, Amana Heritage Society)

Paper rack. The one in the photograph has a central floral motif painted on a background of tin. Some had panels of embroidery. Others had wooden cut-out work of primarily curvilinear lines within a frame. (Courtesy, Amana Heritage Society)

A religious saying of Christian Metz, 1846. (Courtesy, Amana Heritage Society)

*Hand-embroidered religious mottoes and biblical verses were
used as wall accessories. Translated, the message is "Where love
lives there is God's blessing." (Courtesy, Amana Heritage Society)*

plain, unadorned frames of walnut or cherry with mitered
corners could be seen occasionally, with a painting of fruit
or flowers by Joseph Prestele, a well-known Amana artist
whose interest in horticulture in Munich attracted the interest and financial support of the Duke of Bavaria in Pres-

This framed Lord's Prayer in German was executed in colored thread and used as a wall accessory. (Courtesy, Amana Heritage Society)

tele's early years. This led him to a later career in lithography outside the Amana community.[3] In the 1930s the paintings of Carl Flick, John Noe, and others also gained considerable acclaim both within and beyond the boundaries of the villages of Amana. The subjects of their works included buildings, street scenes, and the countryside. Since that time several other local artists have become prominent.

Prestele box. This box was handcrafted of walnut burl overlay by Joseph Prestele. (Courtesy, Dan Berger)

Interior of Prestele box. The lithograph on the inner side of the lid is a Prestele original. The message Zum Andenken means "for remembrances or keepsakes" and is printed below the image. (Courtesy, Dan Berger)

Two styles of tables were predominant in Amana homes. One was a simple square table that had round tapered legs with a small amount of ball turning below the apron and just above the foot. White casters were placed under the table legs that could accommodate them. Early tables of this style had one or two drawers. The second style, which was a little more ornate with molding or turning, was a five- or six-legged gateleg table that could be extended on one side with a leaf. The table was placed against a wall of the living room and covered with a table-cloth of drawnwork or an embroidered runner and accessorized with a potted green plant; it was treated more as a decorative than a functional piece.

Ebenezer and early Amana table. Tables of this basic style were undoubtedly transported from New York to Iowa. Others were made in Amana. Each had a fixed top; one drawer, usually with a porcelain pull or turned wooden mushroom pull; and slightly tapered legs with some ring turning.

The Inspirationists had come from a part of the world where clock making was important. They liked clocks, and nearly every living room had one on the wall. Some of the early clocks had come from Europe; some were purchased from dealers in the East. Probably more individuality and creativeness were evident in this art form than in any other. There was much latitude in the kinds of chimes and strikes and in the lengths of running time. The cases of walnut and cherry frequently had finials, carving, molding, rosettes, and applied spindles in addition to the more traditional straight lines and recessed panels on the sides. Some clocks were housed in glass domes, and small clocks, like present-day travel clocks, were frequently on the bedside table of

Old Amana traditional gateleg table with porcelain casters. The components of the drawers have dovetail joints. The legs are joined to the frame by mortise-and-tenon joints. (Courtesy, Connie Zuber)

The Ebenezer-style headboard. This style headboard was popular. It can be found in most of the showrooms today. (Courtesy, Krauss Furniture and Clock Factory)

the father of the family. The head of the household had the Sunday morning chore of winding the clocks with seven-day movements. The special interest in clocks and clock making perhaps had some origination in the fact that the people of Amana prided themselves on being on time.

A family may also have been fortunate to have a rolltop desk, corner cupboard, or open-type china closet—a few had been brought from Germany. This kind of piece was the exception rather than the rule.

The furniture of the bedroom usually consisted of two single beds, a commode, a washstand, a night table, and a side chair or two. The beds were of a variety of designs; however, the headboards and footboards generally were of the same height and were of solid wood paneling. One exception is the style commonly referred to as "Ebenezer," with a small amount of openness on both the headboard and footboard next to the corner posts. The beds were shorter than the beds on the commercial market today. Mattresses of horsehair were supported by ropes that were knotted in a square pattern and attached to the frame by pegs. Feather ticks were used as a covering for warmth, and

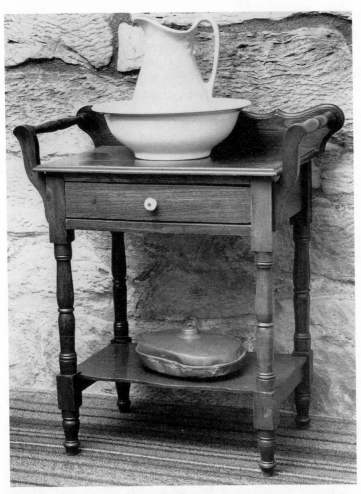

Amana pine washstand. It is approximately thirty-four inches high and has a rectangular top. The gallery at the back is curvilinear and the ends serve as a support for towel bars on each side. Washstands usually had one drawer with a porcelain or wooden mushroom turned pull. The legs have baluster turning with square sections at the top. A bed warmer is shown on the lower shelf. (Courtesy, Amana Heritage Society)

natural, undyed calico fabric was made into bed linens. The beds were placed parallel to the sides of the room, with a night table beside the husband's bed. The small square table had a plain apron and four round, tapered legs, each with a small amount of turning. The washstand resembled the night table in general shape and characteristics but was taller and had a supported wooden rod on either side for a towel. The flat surface on the top held a large basin and pitcher for water.

When a baby was born, a cradle was added. This piece, which was often passed along to families as needed, was much more elaborate in design than the simple lines so evident in much of the furniture. The rockers were removable so the cradle could be used later as a stationary baby bed. There were chairs for children similar in design to those used by adults. And there were nursing chairs with cham-

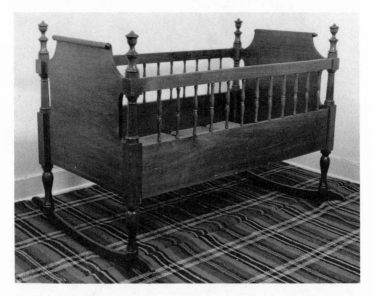

Baby cradle. The rockers are removable so that the cradle can be converted to a crib. It rests on an Amana woven rag carpet. The carpet was usually woven with a striped rather than a plaid pattern. (Courtesy, Connie Zuber)

*Nursing chair. A conven-
ience for young and old.*

ber pots for the children as well as for the aged. A variety of
wooden toys, such as rocking horses, wagons, carts, doll
beds, building blocks, sleds, and small chairs, were made
either by the cabinetmaker or by those interested in
woodworking as a pastime.

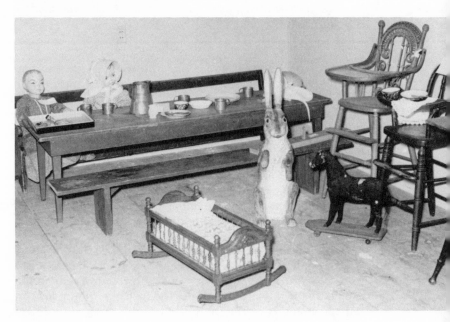

*Children's furniture and toys. (Photographic Collection, Amana
Heritage Society)*

A wooden chest used for storage. (Courtesy, Amana Heritage Society)

Barbara Hoehnle wrote that the wooden moving and storage boxes that had been assembled in Ebenezer with the use of dovetail joints were made later into furniture to be used as *Schränke,* or storage chests. She described other wooden chests called *Brandkiste:* "From the outside they looked like a simple box with two doors and perhaps handles which would allow someone to pick up the chest and move it more easily. These chests were used to store garments, papers, and perhaps more valuable items so that if a fire would break out in the home, the chest could be picked up and removed from the building, hence the word 'Brand' or burn."[4]

The bride-to-be of a cabinetmaker was often favored by special gifts, such as a handcrafted, hand-rubbed wooden box, a *Schatullche,* of cherry or walnut with a hinged lid. Since this box was symbolic of the love of a young artisan for his sweetheart, the front and lid were frequently inlaid with contrasting woods in stylized designs of objects of nature such as birds or fruit. The young woman was also more fortunate than others in that her fiancé would frequently create a piece of furniture that was more elaborate in design.

A handcrafted, hand-rubbed wooden box for a sweetheart. (Courtesy, Ferdinand and Henrietta Ruff)

Just as the women in the kitchen wanted to maintain a fine reputation for their cooking, the cabinetmaker was justly proud of his work and wanted beautiful furniture in his home. He frequently made a special effort to create pieces of unusual design with combinations of woods, carving, and inlay. Many pieces were made of solid woods; other cherished pieces were created with veneered surfaces that gave a uniqueness to the design and added strength. Close friends of the cabinetmaker were sometimes favored in a similar fashion. Such specially made furniture has been handed down from one generation to the next. All of this serves to enhance the appeal of the design and decorative quality of Amana furniture, then and now.

Outdoor Furniture

The combination of an abundance of wood and men with a strong work ethic gave impetus to the building of considerable outdoor furniture—trellises, fences, lamp posts, railings, milk boxes, birdhouses, platform yard swings, and outdoor benches. All were executed with the same dedication as the indoor furniture.

The exterior facades of the grayed and plain clapboard houses were enhanced with a series of vertical and horizontal wooden slats attached at right angles and parallel to the sides of the structures. These trellises extended from the foundation to a foot or so above the top of the first floor windows and could be found on all four sides of most houses, schools, meetinghouses, and hotels and on some businesses. They provided points of attachment for the abundant grapevines or an occasional climbing rose.

Credit for the introduction of trellises is given to Joseph Prestele, the artist and horticulturist, probably because of his strong interest in fruit and flowers and his sense of orderliness. He is also believed to have been the originator of the *Rabatte*, an elevated garden area approximately two feet in width, adjacent and parallel to the lines of the exterior foundation of the houses. The soil of the planting bed was held in place by wood in the early days. Later, in some instances, the wood was replaced by concrete. The trellises and *Rabatten* with their varied plantings added decorative touches to otherwise plain facades.[5]

Fences made of three unpainted horizontal boards and square posts separated house from house, house from street, and house from business. The fence would end near the entrance of a house, where a lamp post would support a kerosene lamp. This was the only street lighting for members of a society of early risers and nightly churchgoers. Wooden-board walkways between the fences and roadways created more uniformity and orderliness, and were the sounding boards for endless footsteps morning and evening. The walkways were practical; built over an occasional drainage ditch parallel to the road, they accommodated the many walkers during wet weather, and they served well as all-season pathways.

Years earlier, *Werkzeug* Barbara Heinemann established through a revelation that Inspirationists should not have flowering or ornamental plantings but only fruit-bearing trees in their lawns. (It is interesting to note the continued wide use of flowers in outside gardens despite the injunction. Today the look of discipline is carried into the trim lawns bordered with well-manicured plots of vegetables and rows of nostalgic, old-fashioned flowers such as zinnias, marigolds, and four o'clocks.)

The Inspirationists had a great appreciation for flora and fauna and made considerable effort to teach their children to treasure all that nature provided. Birdhouses atop tall poles provided suitable housing for families of purple martins.

An occasional lawn would have a wooden platform yard swing—a favorite of anyone who has been fortunate enough to have had the opportunity to glide back and forth on one. The swings and lawn benches were made of a series of unpainted wooden slats put into place by the handyman of the household or possibly by the cabinetmaker. An occasional windmill, hand pump, and metal boot scraper completed the outdoor scene.

Collections of Historic Furniture

Numerous examples of German-inspired Ebenezer- and Amana-made furniture and furnishings can be seen in the Amana villages today. The Amana Heritage Museum in Amana and the Communal Kitchen and the Coopershop museums in Middle Amana, all under the sponsorship of the Amana Heritage Society, have excellent examples of items that were in typical Amana homes of an earlier day. A privately owned furniture museum, which is housed in a former meetinghouse in West Amana, has some examples of old Amana furniture, along with other American period furniture.

One of the several dining rooms at the oldest restaurant in Amana, the Colony Inn, is furnished with an interesting type of sturdy side chair. It has a plank seat and a straight back pierced with a heart motif commonly used by the

Amana "Dutch" chair. This style chair originated in Europe and is still in use in inns there. In Amana it is used in one of the dining rooms at the Colony Inn Restaurant. (Courtesy, Walter and Florence Schuerer)

Pennsylvania Germans. This chair is a version of the *sgabello*, a chair form originating in the sixteenth century in Europe and later popular in inns and eating establishments. These seating pieces were made in the Society-owned Amana Furniture Shop by Amana cabinetmakers. In Amana these are referred to as "Dutch" chairs.

Many historically interesting pieces of furniture are privately owned and can be found in Amana homes. Among these is the Christian Metz chair. The underside of the seat of this chair has the dated, inscribed signatures of Metz and each descendant who has inherited the chair. A Barbara Heinemann chair has been donated to the Amana Heritage Museum collection.

Christian Metz chair. This chair was made especially for and used by the Werkzeug, *Christian Metz. (Courtesy, Theo and Helen Kippenhan)*

Underside of the Christian Metz chair. This chair has been handed down to the descendants of the Werkzeug. *Each person receiving the chair has signed and dated the bottom. (Courtesy, Theo and Helen Kippenhan)*

The Ox Yoke and Ronneburg restaurants, both located in Amana, have special rooms in which furniture of historical significance, such as chairs, wardrobes, tables, and other pieces, are displayed. The Amana Barn Restaurant, built with many exposed timbers from an old Society barn, has paper-backed Amana woven woolen fabric on the walls of the barroom and an Amana-made clock and display case in the lobby.

A fine example of an early horsehair-padded sofa, a church bench, tables, and numerous other interesting items can be seen at Bill Zuber's Restaurant and Gifts, Inc., in Homestead. This enterprise is housed in a large brick building built in 1862; it served as a village hotel for many of the early years. It is also interesting to note that the business was established by a native of Middle Amana of Swiss-German descent who was a major league baseball player in spite of the fact that during his youth baseball was not considered a favorable activity by the Elders.[6]

The oldest general store is the one located in High Amana; it was built in 1858, and the interior has not been changed through the years. Antique shops scattered throughout the villages carry items that were found in typical Amana homes.

CHAPTER 6

Furniture Design

The origin of the design of the furniture created and built by the Amana craftsmen is obscure. The design was undoubtedly influenced by the European and German background and later by the American environment in Ebenezer and Amana.

The Inspirationists sought isolation from worldly influence in all aspects of daily life. Such societies are often characterized by a considerable degree of uniformity. Professor Grace Chaffee expressed this idea: "Physical and sentimental isolation from the world, a unified attitude toward its own exclusive experience, and an emphasis upon primitive Christianity, with simplicity of thought and behavior, affects every aspect of life. The product of the craftsman and cabinetmaker partakes of this general tendency."[1]

Many of the Inspirationists possessed and eventually transported to Amana one or more pieces of furniture of various types that had been used in their homes before the move to the castles, cloisters, and estates in Hesse. These "treasured pieces" can be seen in Amana homes today. Some have elaborate inlay, with a combination of different woods and a relatively large amount of ornamentation. The cabinetmakers of that period of European history were highly skilled.

The furniture of the 1800s in Germany and Europe did

Commode brought from Germany in about 1842. This piece, along with several others shown in this chapter, belonged to members of the Winzenried family, owners of the Winzenried Woolen and Stocking Factory in Lieblos, Germany, at the time they decided to join the Inspirationists. The factory was in full operation as early as 1750. (Courtesy, Connie Zuber)

not reflect any new strong cultural, economic, or political influences, as had been the case during the reigns of Louis XIV, Louis XV, and Louis XVI of France. At this time in Germany many details of earlier forms were being imitated and incorporated into desks, chairs, chests of drawers, tables, and beds. The Biedermeier style—a mix of classical Sheraton, Regency, Directoire, and French Empire influences—affected furniture forms. Some pieces of furniture displayed an honest simplicity; others were enriched with more ornamentation and detail.

The aristocracy and royalty, as well as some wealthy commoners, utilized the services of designers and skilled

A beautiful old maple rocker from Germany, also brought to America by the Winzenried family in about 1842. (Courtesy, Connie Zuber)

cabinetmakers, which allowed them to have the best furniture designs. The less privileged portion of the population could not afford such furniture and had to be satisfied with more provincial designs built by less skilled craftsmen who were often primarily carpenters.

The medieval furniture of the cloisters, in which many Inspirationists lived while in Hesse, was plain and functional. The simplicity undoubtedly influenced the furniture design found in Amana today. Religious prohibitions against ostentatious living were also important.

The migration of the eight hundred Inspirationists to the United States brought them into contact with an environment that differed radically from their European homeland. Christian Metz and four companions were the first to be exposed to this change when they sought a suitable place for the Inspirationists to settle. They spent five days in New York and then moved on to the Mansion House, a hotel in Buffalo, where they stayed for many weeks.[2] There were subsequent visits to other cities and rural areas. This exposure to living conditions and styles that were significantly different undoubtedly had a major impact. Chris-

tian Metz, the carpenter and cabinetmaker, might well have
noticed differences in the structural and decorative designs
of the furniture.

*Secretary. This imposing piece was brought from Germany in
about 1842. The cabinetmaker incorporated numerous construction techniques and kinds of wood. The interior has many secret
compartments and other divisions of varying sizes. (Courtesy,
Connie Zuber)*

The cabinetmakers among the Inspirationists who followed were influenced in a similar fashion. They did not
forget the designs with which they worked in Hesse, but
they gradually incorporated the ideas and techniques of
their new environment. Their relative isolation gave them
little access to design changes and innovations taking place
in Europe. As new generations of cabinetmakers evolved,
some of the methods for training new craftsmen began to
depart from those used in Hesse, which further influenced
the furniture design.

Particular whims and attitudes within a religious sect
play a role. The people of Amana tended to shun color. The

*Chest. The Winzenried family brought this chest from Germany
in about 1842. Much of its beauty is derived from the simple structural design and the matching panels. (Courtesy, Connie Zuber)*

Youth chair, ca. 1890, one adaptation of the spindle-back chair handcrafted in Amana. The traditional Amana woven carpet was used in homes and meetinghouses.

houses were unpainted, the furniture was finished in natural tones, and the clothing was dark. The only colors in their lives were the wide expanse of the blue sky over the prairie, nature's flowers, and the "colony blue" walls of their homes. This was in part a result of scarcity on the frontier, the social cohesiveness of the group, and the attempt to be self-sufficient—all based on the idea that individuals were to subordinate themselves to their religion and that earthly affairs were not to distract them from their primary purpose in life.

The furniture design of the Inspirationists was partly patterned to meet the rigors of the frontier. It was simple, utilitarian, and relatively unadorned. Members were concerned with the bare necessities of life; they bypassed the artistic for the religious. Chaffee states,

> The sectarian community, then, offers two keys for the translation and appreciation of its culture. One is that crises, such as migrations, tend to add new ingredients to the traditional elements of its organization. The other is that adaptations arise because of the life that must be lived under conditions set by the community itself. One influence comes from without; the other, from within. These two tendencies, operating upon the native culture of the group, give the furniture and household articles of the sectarian community their own peculiar flavor and personality.[3]

Drop-leaf table. The style of this repaired and refinished walnut table with curved drop leaves is similar to tables crafted by the early cabinetmakers. The center leaf is fixed, and there are no drawers. The decorative qualities lie in the plainness, some ring turning on the straight legs, and the graining of the wood. (Courtesy, Schanz Furniture and Refinishing Shop)

Like the Inspirationists, other religiously oriented groups of people emigrated from Europe and established cooperative societies. Among these were the Amish, Harmonists, Mennonites, Moravians, Pennsylvania Germans, Separatists, and Shakers. Most were laborers or peasants seeking a simple life with religious freedom, an equality among individuals, and security in attaining the basic needs of life without frills and frivolity.

The Moravians, who were organized in Hesse much earlier than the Inspirationists, lived in the same Marienborn Castle, then migrated to Bethlehem, Pennsylvania, and in 1753 moved to Salem, North Carolina. Since the two groups had similar ethnic backgrounds and had experienced life on an American frontier, it might be expected that their furniture would have been similar, but this was not the case. While Inspirationist furniture had straight structural lines, the Moravians incorporated more ornateness, more carving, painted decoration, and glazing. They also encouraged trade with communities as far away as Charleston, South Carolina, that were becoming important cabinetmaking centers. The Moravians apparently emphasized the professionalism of cabinetmaking and attracted other skilled cabinetmakers from surrounding communities.[4] These influences from the external world gave rise to design changes in Moravian furniture and a departure from the original simplicity.

The Pennsylvania Germans lived in greater isolation and maintained their simple structural designs, much like in the Amanas. But they created a folk art in decorative design. Chests were painted, chair backs pierced, and motifs such as tulips, hearts, birds, flowers, and stars gave a unique and characteristic appearance to the creations of this group of people.

The Shaker society was also a communal society. Both the Shakers and the Inspirationists were self-sufficient, with all outside business and contacts being made by the trustees or Elders. Worldly influence was minimal. The furniture design of the Shakers, even more than that of Amana, reflects a life-style of plainness, honesty, orderliness, perfection, and purity and has become a classical American style used in country and contemporary settings.

Early Amana sofa. Many sofas of the late 1800s had no uphol-stery on the backs and arms. This piece, made in Middle Amana, has been refinished and reupholstered. Some who possess sofas of this style have chosen to add arm pillows and a long, loose cushion to the back. (Courtesy, Connie Zuber)

The design and tradition of Shaker furniture will continue to be popular; Shaker society, which was founded on the cornerstone of celibacy, may soon be only history.

Not all communal societies developed unique furniture designs. There were a variety of reasons. For example, some groups did not have skilled cabinetmakers, suitable hardwoods were not always readily available, and many of these immigrants did not have extensive exposure to European furniture styles. Some of these societies were primarily engaged in subsistence farming and resided in rough-hewn houses in which fine furniture was out of place.

The societies that developed their own unique styles of furniture generally adapted their European experiences with furniture to particular social and religious needs and the demands of the new American environment. Adaptations in form and detail occurred as the artisans reproduced old designs in new furniture. The isolation in which many of these people lived gave them few designs to copy and

Schrank, *a piece of furniture used for storage, either as a wardrobe or trunk. This piece is a reproduction of a Schrank made in Amana by an Amana cabinetmaker generations ago. (Courtesy, Amana Furniture Shop)*

reproduce. Furniture styles that were not greatly influenced by American designs emerged. An exception was the furniture style of the Moravians, who adopted designs then in vogue in the furniture centers of the Carolinas. Others such as the Pennsylvania Germans introduced new ideas from within.

The people of Amana possessed many pieces of fine furniture crafted in their European homeland. They brought highly skilled cabinetmakers in the move from Hesse to the United States. The Elders recognized the importance of passing these skills to the next generation through apprenticeship and training. Also important was the existence of an adequate supply of hardwoods in the surrounding timberland.

Amana families retained the European pieces in their homes, but furniture of much simpler structural and decorative design was developed. The religious ban on ostentation was one reason. Economy in the utilization of labor dictated by the scarcities of early frontier living was also important. The result was a furniture style that was neither European nor American, but uniquely Amana.

The basic design of an Amana chest or table was essentially the same year after year. Straight lines and simplicity predominated. Chests and wardrobes (*Schränke*) had rectilinear lines, with recessed panels on the front and ends. Most tables were square or rectangular with square tapered legs. Five-legged gateleg tables with one drop leaf and turned legs had some similarity to the refectory tables found in castles and cloisters in Hesse and elsewhere. Four-legged stools and benches were popular; every sitting room had a low footstool of simple lines. The only exceptions among the handcrafted pieces were the few decorative items requested by the friends of the cabinetmaker.

CHAPTER 7

The Cabinetmaker in Communal Amana

The religious concepts of the Inspirationists found expression in the creative hands of those who worked with wood.[1] The simple, functional, and utilitarian characteristics of the furniture reflected the disciplined devotion of a people to their doctrines of unworldliness and godliness. The Society artisans maintained high standards and sought a perfection and a beauty that has continued as a part of the Amana tradition today. They believed, as John Ruskin did, that devotion to God and nature was primary; form must be related to function without excess decoration or superfluous ornamentation. As Ruskin wrote, "Leave your walls bare as a planed board, or build them of baked mud and chapped straw, if need be; but do not rough-cast them with falsehood."[2]

The Training

The Elders were the temporal as well as the spiritual leaders of the Society. As such, they were concerned with the economic development of the villages and the allocation of human resources. When the need for a new cabinetmaker arose, the Elders generally selected a young man who had shown an interest and aptitude for the craft. One young man who was chosen had shown a talent for woodworking at an early age by making picture frames. Another helped his cabinetmaker uncle. Others showed their interest by stopping by the cabinet shop after school and helping with small tasks such as puttying windows.

There were times when the Elders and the young man did not agree on the choice of a trade or profession. For example, one young man who was anxious to become a dentist, doctor, or teacher became a store manager because of community need. However, a boy who had been selected for another vocation in spite of his interest in woodworking successfully convinced the Elders he ought to become a Society cabinetmaker.

The apprentice program began immediately following graduation from eighth grade. The young apprentices worked alongside the seasoned craftsmen day after day, accepting their words of wisdom and imitating their skills. In some villages there was only one senior cabinetmaker, while in others there were three or four.[3] Apprentices assumed such extra duties as sweeping out the wood shavings and running errands, but the general responsibilities were shared. They concentrated on learning the skills of cabinetmaking. Gradually the apprentice became a skilled craftsman, with no special recognition or ceremony to mark the end of the training period and the beginning of full-fledged cabinetmaking.

The Daily Work Routine

Cabinetmakers, along with the other men and working boys, ate breakfast in the community kitchen, then proceeded to the cabinet shop to begin the day's work. During the middle of the morning work period the cabinetmakers, as well as those in other pursuits, walked to the community kitchen for a midmorning lunch of homemade bread, jam, cheese, and coffee. After eating they returned to their workbenches and the smell of fresh-cut lumber. The bell in the *Glockenhaus* rang out at 11:30 A.M. to announce that the noon meal was ready to be served in the kitchens. The shop was closed and the workers returned to their respective homes to wash, then went to the kitchen to eat, returned home for a few minutes of relaxation, and went back to work. The afternoon work period was also relieved by a half-hour lunch between 2:30 and 3:00 P.M.—again a lunch of bread, cheese, jam, and coffee. The normal work day ended at 5:30 P.M., just in time to return to the kitchen, eat, and be ready for the evening church services at 7:00 P.M. There were no time clocks or eight-hour days; the men of the Society willingly gave of themselves and worked overtime when it was necessary. Working conditions were made as pleasant as possible and work was considered a joy. There were no monetary rewards for additional work; if the hours were demanding and excessive, the men were given credits that could be redeemed at the general store for items not normally provided to the families by the Society.

Cabinetmakers worked every day except Saturday afternoons, Sundays, and church and national holidays. During periods when the farmers or others required help because of the pressure of work or weather, the labor force was shifted to meet these needs. Changes or revisions in work assignments were handed out by the Elders each evening following church services. Cabinetmakers could easily be temporarily assigned to plow the corn, milk the cows, assist with dredging the canal, care for the threshing machine, or help with the cutting of ice from the Iowa River. The bulk of the cabinetmaking was carried on during the winter months and in inclement weather; the shop was heated by means of a potbellied stove. Cabinetmakers did not retire at a specific age; they worked as long as they were able. Work was meaningful and pleasant.

The Cabinet Shop

Each village of the Amana Society had its own cabinet shop, or *Schreinerei*. The workshop usually consisted of two rooms or more: an assembling room, a paint room for varnishing, and in the larger shops an additional room for the machinery. In some instances the rooms were side by side, separated only by a door; in one village the workroom was on the first floor of the building and the paint room was

Early cabinet shop in Amana. It is now part of the Amana Furniture Shop. (Photographic Collection, State Historical Society of Iowa)

on the second floor. It was necessary to have some separation to prevent wood dust from settling on the newly finished surfaces. The rooms had several small-paned, double-hung windows to provide adequate light for the artisans and their exacting work.

The cabinetmakers and the apprentices in the shops were each provided with a workbench, an apron, and a set of small tools. Attached to the wall in back of the workbench was a cabinet with doors to house the tools. Within the cabinet was a series of shelves approximately sixteen inches deep that were notched along the front edge so that the various tools could be hung in an orderly fashion. The cabinet doors had locks, but the keys in the keyholes were never turned. The cabinetmaker usually preferred to stand rather than sit while he worked. Some of the original workbenches are still in use.

The tools of the shop were those well known to cabinet-makers of the day. Some were brought from Germany; others were locally made. They included all kinds of saws, a complete set of bits for the drill, gimlets, augers, squares, chisels, rasps, wooden clamps, hammers, mallets, spoke-haves, scrapers, dividers (or compasses), screwdrivers, awls, miter boxes, and vises. There were jointer, jack, smoothing, rapid, and router planes. All tools were hand-powered except the difficult-to-operate pedal sander and the lathe, which was steam-powered or propelled by horse power. The nearby non-Inspirationist farmers of Iowa County knew the cabinetmakers had foot-propelled stone

Workbench of the late 1800s. Even though this workbench is approximately a hundred years old, it is still in daily use and is very functional. The only change is the addition of electrical outlets. (Courtesy, Krauss Furniture and Clock Factory)

wheels for sharpening their tools, so they would bring along axes and blades to be sharpened when making trips to the Amanas for grinding grain or purchasing supplies from the general store.

Hand tools, dating from 1805, used by early cabinetmakers in the Schanz family. (Courtesy, Schanz Furniture and Refinishing Shop)

Patterns for the curved areas of the furniture were cut from wood of lesser quality. No patterns were used for the straight forms; these measurements were marked with a pencil on a lathlike stick called the "pattern stick." Dowels were made by forcing wooden pegs through an iron form. Such techniques as dovetailing and the making of mortise-and-tenon joints were common in the Amana workshops.

The Materials

Since the Community of True Inspiration was a self-supporting, independent community, most of the materials used in the cabinet shops were produced or obtained within the boundaries of the villages. An adequate source of fine timberland for building materials as well as for fuel and furniture had been one of the priorities in the decision to move from Ebenezer. The abundance of this resource along the Iowa River and upper hills proved a valuable asset.

The sawmill was erected early as a village started to take shape. It was to be central to the construction of new buildings and located within one thousand feet of the cabinet shop. A durable roof to protect it from the weather was put in place as soon as time and labor could be delegated to the task.

The wood for the cabinet shop was cut in the fall into long lengths and transferred by the timber crews on low wagons or sleighs to a yard near the cabinet shop. The logs were stored over the winter. In the spring they were stripped, sawed, and put into a shed or hay loft where the air could circulate and age the wood. This process would be continued for five years, fifteen years, or even twenty years. The cabinetmaker liked the wood to dry slowly so that a certain amount of the sap would remain. The wood of the trees grown on the bluffs was preferred because it contained less moisture and was not so likely to warp and split. The lumber from trees grown in the valleys would likely have been subjected to an occasional flooding and consequently would show more graining. The species varied; walnut was considered choice, and a wood referred to as "whitewood," though greenish in color, was very popular.[4]

The beauty of Amana furniture is largely in its simple lines and hand-rubbed finish. The only metal adornments were the plain and functional hinges attached to the reverse side of the doors, and the escutcheons, locks, and keys. The locksmiths of the respective villages made the metal components and an occasional handle for a chest.

The varnish of the earlier days was a homemade preparation with linseed oil as the base. This finish is now identifiable by its crackled surface. Later, varnish was purchased from the outside. The finishing process that developed included sanding, filling, and applying an undercoat and three coats of varnish. After the varnish had dried, the surface was rubbed with rottenstone and paraffin oil.

Most of the other materials used in the cabinet shop were obtained from outside. Materials such as glue and upholstery fabric for any of the individual cabinet shops were ordered through the Amana Society office. The glue, which was purchased from a nearby meat processing plant, was obtained in sheets or flakes, which were later melted and heated to the boiling point to secure an adequate adhesive. The harness maker supplied horsehair for the sofa padding.

Other Duties of Cabinetmakers

In addition to making furniture for the homes and fulfilling occasional irregular assignments from the Elders, cabinetmakers were expected to carry out a variety of other woodworking duties. These included repairing eaves and siding and replacing window frames. In South Amana one of the cabinetmakers also served as a plumber and laid the water lines.

Another responsibility was that of making coffins. When a Society member died, the cabinetmaker would go to the home of the deceased, measure the body with the length of a stick, and proceed immediately to make a pine box. The lengthwise boards were joined by means of wooden pegs. The lid, which was hinged by wooden pins, consisted of three long planks angled in a flat-gabled fashion. The earlier coffins probably had a wooden handle on each side and, when closed, were topped with flat boards that were held in place with wooden dowels. Within a day the burial box was smoothed, stained a rich dark brown, and taken "home."

The cabinetmakers made the furniture for the church and communal kitchens. The meetinghouse was architecturally austere and the furniture within equally so. The same was true of the furniture in the communal kitchens.

Community Use of Tools

Many men of the community who had tools available to them found woodworking a pleasant hobby and a means for providing extra pieces of furniture for their families and toys for their children. Grandfathers made wooden wagons and carts for grandchildren; husbands made whatnot shelves and paper racks for their homes. Items of furniture were popular Christmas gifts. Woodworking activities served not only as a productive function but as a religious one, for to keep the mind occupied was to keep it free from ideas of worldliness.

CHAPTER 8

The Clockmaker

The story of the early Amana cabinetmakers would not be complete without the contributions of another craftsman whose work was closely related to that of the cabinetmaker—the clockmaker. Frederick Hahn of Middle Amana was such a craftsman.[1] Hahn was born in Langenselbold in Hesse and came with his family directly to Amana from Germany. As a curious young man of fourteen, Hahn constantly explored new ways of doing things. In 1857, when ready for his first work assignment, the Elders of his village placed him in the machine shop of the Amana Woolen Mill. Hahn gained a wide range of mechanical and technical expertise that soon served interests beyond the requirements of his job. He then became a land surveyor at a time when boundaries needed definition.

This active young man had an accident with a horse and wagon and was unable to continue strenuous outdoor activity. His talents led him to working with wood and making beautiful handcrafted chairs and other pieces of furniture as well as wooden toys for children, such as rocking horses and doll houses. Among many other achievements, he made a violin, even though musical instruments were still prohibited. Hahn also played a major role in developing the technical aspects of the telephone system in Amana. This led him to make most of the wall-mounted oak cases

Frederick Hahn constructed many toys for the children of the community. These included rocking horses, wagons, sleds, wheelbarrows, miniature animals, chairs, tables, and Klicker-bahn. (Courtesy, Marvin and Emaline Bendorf)

for home and business telephones—the telephones with a crank on the right for calling the operator, two shiny exposed silver bells on the top, a mouthpiece and small shelf in front, and a long black tubular receiver suspended on a hook on the left side.

Hahn was renowned as a cabinetmaker, but through the years he became better known for his clockmaking, a craft that required a combination of mechanical and cabinetmaking skills. His creations were assembled with such integrity of design and workmanship that many of his clocks are still chiming in Amana homes today.

Little is known about how Frederick Hahn learned the

art of clockmaking. Perhaps his curiosity and creativeness led him to explore the internal workings of a family clock. The Amana Society had a subscription to *Scientific American*, which further stimulated his interest in science and mechanics. His desire to learn was such that Hahn made special arrangements to pick up each issue at the post office as soon as it arrived. After reading an issue he would take it to the Amana bookbinder, who bound it for permanent storage as a future reference.

By the middle of the nineteenth century, when the Inspirationists came to America, the technology of clockmaking was highly developed. Every European village and royal court had its own official town clockmaker. The larger towns had many of these craftsmen. The clockmaker enjoyed a special status in the community, since handmade timepieces provided the only means for knowing the exact time of day. Clocks were installed in churches to mark the times of services and became increasingly important in business and daily life. The significant role played by clocks and clockmaking in the Amana Society can at least partly be traced to a European background. A further consideration was that clocks were playing a greater part in the American frontier, both functionally and aesthetically.

A great number of the clocks made by Hahn were similar in design to those of the well-known Vienna Regulator clocks of Europe, produced in Vienna primarily between 1800 and 1900. The typical Vienna Regulator was a hanging wall clock, three to six feet tall and approximately one and one-half feet wide. The design of the door on the front and the two wood-framed side panels was fairly standard, while the detail of the matching or coordinated carving at the top and bottom of the wooden clockcase would vary, thus identifying the individual Austrian cabinetmaker-clockmaker.

The clocks made by Frederick Hahn were built one at a time, and no two handcrafted Hahn clocks are identical. Most have the same structural design, though there exist some variations in the details of the hand-chiseled decorative design at the top. Walnut seems to have been his favorite wood for the cases; only one clock is reported to have been made of pine.

An original Frederick Hahn clock. (Courtesy, Marvin and Emaline Bendorf)

An identifying characteristic of the mechanisms is the manner in which the round dials were placed on the wooden backplate. The pendulums usually had plain black wooden shafts with handmade round brass bobs to regulate the timing apparatus. The clockmaker used dials and hands that he made or purchased from American clock manufacturers; other moving parts were also purchased and then combined with wheels and levers of Hahn's making. An interesting sidelight is that many clockmakers of the nineteenth century attempted to create a vertical balance in design on the face of clocks by using Roman Numeral IIII to balance with Roman Numeral VIII rather than using the standard IV. Most of the clocks were powered by gravity pulling on lead weights.

Hahn built his clocks at a workbench in a corner of the bedroom in his home. Each morning after making the bed and tidying the bedroom, his wife Louise would cover the bedding with a large white sheet to help keep it free from metallic or wood dust that might be produced by his work. The lack of shop space may have been the reason he made his clocks at home. It is more likely that, since personal hobbies and activities did not promote the purpose of the Community of True Inspiration and were therefore not sanctioned by the church, he chose to work at home. Too, as an Elder it would probably have been important to keep his private pursuits away from the public eye.

Hahn's initials appear in only one known instance; however, through the years a Hahn-made clock has been and can be readily recognized in Amana by its individual characteristics and superb craftsmanship. It is believed that he made from thirty to fifty hanging wall clocks plus a number of mantel clocks, most of which were given to relatives as wedding presents. Amana church histories show no reporting of Frederick Hahn's clockmaking—a void similar to the absence of the recorded artistic endeavors of Joseph Prestele. Both men were highly skilled, and the products of their talents are greatly cherished today.

The hand skills of the cabinetmaker and clockmaker have been combined in a number of instances. The interest and dexterity seem to be easily transferred from one area of expertise to the other. One older artisan explained that it

Many clocks of this type can be found in Amana homes. The relief carving indicates a Victorian influence. They may have been purchased from retailers-clockmakers in the East; the shelf was handcrafted in Amana. (Courtesy, Zuber's Restaurant)

would take him about twelve hours per clock to make the wood bases, tops, and panels, and equally as long to assemble and sand them before he could begin the finishing and installation of the movements. Some cabinetmakers began their careers as apprentices to clockmakers, while others were apprentices to cabinetmakers. Through the years the Society-owned Amana Furniture Shop and the privately owned Krauss Furniture and Clock Factory have developed clockmaking to such a degree that it is now an integral part of their businesses. Clarence Olswold of Middle Amana, a non-Inspirationist clockmaker of Norwegian rather than German descent, built 1,713 clocks at his workbench in the Amana Furniture Shop before he retired.

CHAPTER 9

From Communal Living to Capitalism

Amajor reorganization, commonly referred to as the "Great Change," occurred in 1932. The covenant for a communal society, which began in the German state of Hesse and reached full fruition in Ebenezer and Amana, was abandoned for a more capitalistic order. The religious side of life was given an organizational identity apart from secular endeavor.

Why the Great Change?

Many forces combined to cause this radical departure from communal living. The charismatic leadership of Christian Metz had played a major role in the development of Amana-style communism. Metz and Bárbara Heinemann, the last two *Werkzeuge*, provided strong religious guidance and support. As Lawrence Rettig wrote, "Without the direction and inspiration of the *Werkzeuge*, religious enthusiasm declined. The spontaneity and fervor of the inspired prophets were gone."[1] The social conformity forged by strong religious beliefs began to give way to individualism and self-interest.

Religious persecution, which caused the move to Ebenezer and Amana, had played a major part in promoting social cohesion and cooperation. The isolation of the

frontier and the more tolerant American society removed
this important reason for a unity of purpose. At the same
time, the external culture and society started to impose new
values. The highly secular American environment began to
play an increasingly important role.

The railroad, which reached Homestead in August
1860, rapidly moved products and people into the surrounding countryside. In 1855, when the Inspirationists began the trek from Ebenezer to Iowa, the population of Iowa
County totaled 2,307. By 1880 the number of county inhabitants had increased to 19,221.[2] A pioneer reported that in
1852 the town of Marengo, located a few miles from the
Amana Society, consisted of "fourteen dwellings, two
stores, a blacksmith shop, one hotel, one 1½-story
loghouse. There were but three dwellings built of anything
but logs. There was a small postoffice, a stage station and a
saloon."[3] By 1880 Marengo had a population of 1,738 and a
substantial business and social infrastructure.[4]

As long as horses and oxen provided the primary motive power, a large measure of physical isolation remained
to safeguard the Amana Society from the external world.
The situation became more difficult in the early 1900s
when the automobile and improved roads brought the outside world to the Amanas' very doorstep. Tourists were attracted to the Amana villages; hotels, restaurants, and
shops were established to accommodate them.

During earlier years in both Ebenezer and Amana, the
Inspirationists had experienced the intrusions of the outside world. Christian Metz constantly implored people to
forsake worldliness. Those who abandoned a simplicity of
dress and life-style were often severely admonished. Metz
regarded the desire to live according to the latest fashion as
a human frailty to be overcome at all costs.[5] He believed
that withdrawal from the outside world was the best protection against such sinful behavior.

Young people presented a special problem. In 1857 the
schoolmaster in Ebenezer, Gottfried Mann, complained that
the youth were out of hand and that to make matters worse
the parents often encouraged their children in worldly attitudes.[6] Somewhat later that year, Wilhelm Moershel complained that youths were degenerate and no longer pious.

Metz considered youths in Amana to be difficult and too often indulging in "frivolity and idle love affairs."[7] In many of his letters and writings, Metz expressed concern about failures of the youth to follow the ways of God rather than the world.[8]

Rettig wrote that "the leaders of the Society were faced with a full-blown youth rebellion from the late 1920's until the time of the reorganization in 1932."[9] The temptations and peer pressures of the outside world were too much for many Amana young men and women. The differences between Amana and the society around it became a focal point of controversy. Women began to follow the styles of the day by bobbing their hair, applying lipstick and rouge, and wearing shorter skirts. Movies, jazz music, and ballroom dancing became popular pursuits. Baseball and other games were played on Saturday (the day that had always been reserved for religious study) and even on Sunday afternoon. There were demands to paint the unpainted Amana houses and speak English rather than Amana German.

Many parents gave support to their children through changes in their own attitudes and values. The Sears Roebuck catalog and the stores in neighboring towns flaunted the fashions and life-styles of the external world. People opened personal accounts in outside banks, and a few used their entrepreneurial talents to engage in personal business ventures. A significant number of Amana people began to accept worldliness with the same fervor with which they had once rejected it.

Religious and family-imposed behavioral restraints were no longer as effective as they had been during earlier years. The sanctions of the church became less important to both the youth and older people. Attendance at the eleven church services a week began to decline. Young people no longer viewed exclusion from church services as punishment. Few people were inclined to question the religious mandates imposed by Christian Metz, especially when they came directly from God. After the death of the last two *Werkzeuge,* Christian Metz and Barbara Heinemann, the enforcement of religious and social directives became more difficult.

The breakdown of religious and social bonds had motivational consequences on the economic side. Without the esprit de corps forged by persecution and religious fervor, cooperation and efficiency declined. The benefits of communal living became more important than the corresponding obligations. People began to waste food. The Society doctors were faced with people who feigned illness to escape work. Many refused to work harder or accept more responsibility because their benefits from the Society would not thereby be increased. The lack of productivity of Society workers gave rise to engaging large numbers of hired hands from the outside. At the time of the Change in 1932 more than two hundred outsiders were employed by the Society.

During the earlier years, communal living and work provided important means for contending with the economic scarcities and hardships of the frontier. Amana offered advantages not present in the more individualistic and demanding capitalism on the outside. However, as population increased through immigration and rapid economic development occurred, the surrounding communities began to offer benefits not available in the Amanas.

Amana enterprises became increasingly dependent upon external market forces. The purchase of raw materials and supplies as well as the marketing of Amana products and services reinforced this dependency. The lack of labor productivity, the largesse of the economic and social benefits, and the economic waste began to adversely affect the profitability of Amana enterprises. Also important was that many of the small Amana cottage industries could no longer compete with the efficiencies of mass production.

Amana began to experience economic problems in the 1920s, a time of relative prosperity. The full consequences of this situation became increasingly apparent as the depression of the thirties began to make heavy inroads on Amana income and wealth. Deficits began to appear as early as 1921. Ten years later, during the depth of the depression, the Society was $500,000 in debt and faced serious cash flow problems. Bankruptcy was a distinct possibility, even though the large land holdings and industrial properties had high values.

Amana "communism" had been sustained for many years through strong religious and societal bonds reinforced by the isolation of the frontier. As these bonds became less effective, self-interest became increasingly prevalent and ultimately a highly destructive force. In a society based on altruism, too much self-interest does not serve the common good. On the other hand, capitalism thrives on self-interest and promotes social welfare even though that is not the intent.[10] The superiority of the capitalism practiced in the external society became apparent to Amana Elders. As Peter Stuck, secretary of the Amana Society Corporation, wrote in 1935, "The change was brought about through inherent defects in communism such as inefficiency of communistic labor, lack of the spirit of sacrifice so necessary for successful, voluntary communism, and economic pressure due to the depression, financial losses and the ever increasing burden of taxation."[11]

The early communal living provided an important means for contending with the problems of the past. The change that came in 1932 helped resolve the problems of the future with the same foresight as the earlier decision to adopt communal living. Amana needed to adapt to the cultural, economic, and technological forces of the twentieth century—the same forces that created major changes in the external world. In 1932 there was no longer a frontier to which the Society could move.

The Decision to Change

Many of the problems that ultimately forced change had been a subject of informal discussion among Amana leaders during the 1920s. But a major departure from the communal system put into place by Christian Metz and sanctioned by revelations from God was not something that could be taken lightly. Nothing was done in spite of much talk that change was needed. The depression of the thirties finally forced the issue. The Amana Society was on the road to bankruptcy. Something had to be done. Many of the Elders recognized that change had to come from within and that radical changes in religious, social, and economic relationships were necessary. They wanted the members to remain together rather than to be torn apart. An informal group composed of a number of prominent Amana leaders initiated the process that led to the change.[12]

The Amana Society constitution, which contained no provision for dissolution or change, was amended to include such a provision. The process began with a series of meetings in each of the villages to explain the situation to members.

A letter and a questionnaire in the German language were sent to every Society member. The letter asked for cooperation and indicated the alternatives. The questionnaire consisted of only two choices. One choice was to retain without reservation the old system as originally prescribed. The second asked members to accept the idea of reorganization and cooperation with a plan approved by the trustees and Society members. A deadline of June 10, 1931, was set for the return of the questionnaires.

Of the questionnaires that were distributed, nine hundred were returned. Seventy-five percent of the total membership accepted the idea of reorganizing; twelve percent wanted to retain the old system; the remainder rejected both of the alternatives. There was a strong consensus for change in all of the villages except Middle Amana, where only about twenty-five percent gave a favorable response.

To develop a plan for reorganization, a committee was elected. Committee members could not be members of the *Bruderatt* or of the board of trustees. A total of forty-seven members were elected by the seven villages, with each village being represented in proportion to its population. The committee had a chairman, vice chairman, and secretary as officers, and a number of subcommittees were formed to expedite planning. A proposed plan was presented to the full committee of forty-seven. With the cooperation of the attorney general of Iowa, a detailed plan was developed, and in February 1932 ninety percent of the full membership of the Society voted approval.

The reorganization provided for a separation of the religious and secular spheres. The Amana Church Society was given responsibility for religious and charitable activities. In addition, a capitalistic corporation, the Amana Society, was formed; it had an appraised value of $2,200,000. The members of the original communal society shared through stock ownership.

The formula used to determine the equity of each member in the new Society was described by Arthur Barlow, who was the first business manager:

> The adult years of both male and female members were totaled. The grand total adult years of all members were then divided into the grand total of the Society's assets, less liabilities, which gave the figure evidencing the equity of one adult year. Then by multiplying the number of adult years for each member times the adult year equity, the total equity per member was established and stock issued in said amounts to the members.[13]

The formula assumed that all members, both men and women, had done an equal amount of work irrespective of the tasks that had been performed.

Each member received one share of non-transferable Class A common stock with a book value of fifty dollars, which conferred voting rights controlling the corporation. The owners of this stock were given full medical and dental care and were assured their burial expenses would be paid. The corporation was required to purchase such stock at the death of the owner. Young people could become voting members by purchasing Class A common stock when they reached the age of majority. Outsiders could become owners of common stock by a two-thirds vote of all common stockholders.

In addition, members received nonvoting, transferable stock for the remaining amount of their equity as determined by the above formula. These shares provided security for older members who had accumulated many adult years of service. Many members used this stock to purchase the houses in which they were living.

The governance of the new Amana Society was vested in a board of directors with thirteen members, one from each village and six at large. Each member of the corporation was entitled to cast one vote in a secret ballot. The directors elected the officers of the corporation consisting of a president, vice president, secretary, and treasurer.

Under the laws of the state of Iowa at the time, the Articles of Incorporation had to be renewed in 1952, twenty years after the Change. A charter similar to the original charter of 1932 was presented for the vote of Society members in 1952 and was adopted for another twenty years. A significant change was a provision permitting young people to purchase Class A common stock on an installment basis. However, the approval of the new charter did not mean that all was well.

The problems relating to Class A stock were to split the Society into two competing groups.[14] The result was a long period of antagonism and divisiveness as each side sought to gain its objectives through a series of lawsuits. One problem was the loss of cash flow due to the requirement that the Society had to purchase the Class A stock of deceased members and those who decided to drop their membership. A related problem was the high cost of medical, dental, and burial benefits of the Class A stockholders, many of whom were employed outside the Society.

The method used to determine the value of Class A stock was a major point of controversy. A recommendation that Class A shares be split into more shares with the right to sell such shares to any other person created the fear that the ownership of the Amana Society might be transferred to outsiders. For ten years following 1952, there were a number of plans to resolve the issue, lawsuits and counter suits, and court rulings and reversals. The high costs of litigation added to the financial problems of the Society.

Finally, at a special stockholders' meeting held in 1972, the members decided to return to the basic charter of 1952 with a provision for the issuance of a new type of Class A stock that no longer carried the medical benefits of the old Class A shares. The new shares could be sold to outside parties, but they first had to be offered to the Society for purchase. Restrictions were placed on voting rights to reduce the possibility of outside and minority control. The value of the original Class A shares was adjusted upward through reappraisal.

The date for the next renewal of the Articles of Incorporation was to have been 1992. But late in 1989 the stockholders of the Amana Society approved the adoption of re-

The auction of community kitchen utensils and equipment in West Amana, 1932. (Photographic Collection, Amana Heritage Society. Permission, Rudolph Kellenberger)

vised articles to achieve perpetual corporate status. This was done under Chapter 496A of the Iowa Code, which became law in 1962. The number of board members was reduced from thirteen to nine, and the management structure was adapted to better contend with the demands of the 1990s and beyond. Some have called this development the "Second Great Change."

The Amana Church Society

The religious side of communal Amana was given legal status under the laws of the state of Iowa through a corporation called the Amana Church Society. The constitution, which became effective on December 1, 1932, was signed by members of the original Amana Society.[15] Membership is considered to be a privilege—with religious responsibilities—and not a legal right. The right of the church to remove people from membership and to impose sanctions for nonconformity was not abandoned; however, the religious and social restraints became less stringent than in the past.

The constitution provided for a board of trustees of thirteen to be elected by church members from among the church Elders. The trustees elect the executive officers, including a president, one or more vice presidents, and a treasurer and secretary who can be the same person. All except the secretary and treasurer are required to be board members. Probably the most significant change in governance of the Amana church throughout the years has been a decline in the number of Elders. A peak was reached from 1884 through 1907 with ninety-one Elders, a number that was reduced to sixty-four in 1931. At the time of the Change there were thirty-four Elders; today there are fourteen, including one woman.[16] This reduction has left some villages with no Elders to conduct the services. Consequently, there are now fewer sites for Sunday church services.

In 1935 Peter Stuck, secretary of the new Amana Society corporation, emphasized that the excellent achievements on the business side should not cause a neglect of the religious part of Amana life. He stressed that "Amana—the Church" is also "badly in need of rejuvenation and instilling of new life."[17] In a letter to the editor of the *Amana Society Bulletin,* a weekly publication started in 1932 to inform the residents of business events relating to the Change, a member wrote that "our church, especially, finds it difficult to adapt itself to new conditions. Lack of leadership and interest in church affairs seem to be the greatest drawback here."[18]

In a later *Bulletin,* youths were chided for being too rash and ruthlessly destroying the old principles and traditions of the church. Work on Sunday, improper attire, dancing, and other vestiges of the modern world continued to create problems. A significant number of these differences could be credited to the "generation gap" and matters relating to form rather than fundamental religious beliefs.

The Amana Church Society retained church and school buildings, the cemeteries, and other properties related to its activities. The architecture and interior of the meeting-houses retained their original austere look with the use of the same plain benches outlined against the blue white-washed walls. This physical continuity did not prevent significant changes in other directions.

The old system of ranking church members and services by age and degree of piety was replaced with a common service for all. Services in English began in 1961 to accommodate members who experienced difficulties with Amana German. Many of the social restraints imposed for religious and other reasons upon old and young alike were gradually abandoned. Restrictions against more modern dress, play on Saturday and Sunday, dating and dancing, and other worldly activities were removed.

Religious instruction became the primary responsibility of the church through the establishment of Sunday school, and the public schools became exclusively secular. Education, once formally restricted to the eighth grade, was expanded through attendance at high schools in neighboring towns until an Amana high school could be established. Amana young people began to attend colleges and universities, which served to expand economic opportunities and cultural horizons. Some have played a major role during recent years in stressing the importance of retaining the traditional Amana values.

The social restraints of the early years were liberalized in other directions. Most of the villages organized welfare clubs, which became an important part of socialization for people of all ages. The scope of activities increased gradually and included plays, community picnics, movies, and special holiday parties with musicians providing music for listening or dancing. Entertainment included bingo and betting games; beverages included beer and soft drinks. Some villages erected their own community halls for social activities. Sunday school and Boy Scouts became a part of the life-style.

Toward Amana Capitalism

Most of the people who had occupied leadership positions in the communal system assumed similar roles in the corporation of the new capitalistic order. The thirteen members of the board of directors were all prominent Amana personages. The board created an executive committee from among its members and selected the corporate officers: president, vice president, secretary, and treasurer. An assistant secretary and assistant treasurer were added a short time later. Most of the managers of the departments and enterprises of the communal period continued to play an important part in business and farm operations. The legal work of the Society remained in the hands of outside attorneys.

There was one important exception to the utilization of the old Amana leadership in the new Society. In the fall of 1931 Arthur Barlow, an executive from Cedar Rapids, Iowa, was asked by the executive committee to help make the transition from the old to the new system and to take charge of future business operations.[19] Barlow's background in accounting and finance was highly important during the transition period.

The transition period was officially designated to begin on May 2, 1932, and was not to extend beyond January 1, 1933; however, the steps that needed to be taken to establish the new corporation were begun immediately after the vote of approval on February 1, 1932. For example, in March, Dean Anson Marston of Iowa State College (now University) was asked to make the valuation of Amana industrial properties.[20] This and other valuations were used to establish the worth of the Society for the purposes of accounting and issuing stock in the new Amana Society corporation. They gave rise to authorized capital stock of slightly over two million dollars.

The Change had a major impact on the management and operations of the enterprises of the Amana Society. The profit motive became strategic in agricultural and business enterprises. General and departmental managers began to implement policies that increased revenues and reduced costs. Enterprises that did not have profit potential were immediately or gradually eliminated.

The changes in managerial philosophy brought about an urgent need to measure profit and loss. Arthur Barlow played a major role in emphasizing this need and developing an appropriate accounting system. As Barlow wrote,

"Before the big change, Amana operated in a very decentralized manner from a business standpoint. The new Amana naturally called for a centralized system—one main office, one balance sheet of assets and liabilities, etc."[21]

The managerial activities of the new corporation were conducted in a central office, which was housed in an addition to the Amana general store. It was here that the executive committee of the board and Barlow, the manager, had frequent meetings to consider appropriate strategies for Society development and give direction to the agricultural, business, and industrial operations. There were offices for Barlow and for Peter Stuck and William Moershel, the corporate secretaries, as well as space for a rapidly growing staff of assistants and clerical-secretarial personnel. The high bookkeeping desks and high stools of old Amana were replaced with modern desks and chairs, and the latest office equipment was installed. The managers of the various undertakings sent daily financial and other reports to this office. During monthly and quarterly meetings with departmental and enterprise managers, Barlow emphasized the importance of their profit and loss statements. Barlow reports that they learned quickly to recognize the significance of such data and the results they implied. The practitioners of communal management became capitalistic in short order.

At the beginning there were enterprises of many types and sizes. There were industrial plants such as a flour mill, meat plants, woolen mills; utilities such as a telephone system, water systems, and transport facilities; craft shops such as basket shops, blacksmith shops, a bookbindery, a print shop, harness shops, machine shops, an umbrella shop, and cabinet and carpentry shops; business establishments such as bakeries, hotels, and a lumberyard; agricultural activities such as dairies, a hog operation, grain production, and the maintenance and harvesting of sizable forests. Some of these, such as the wagon, harness, and blacksmith shops, were discontinued, and smaller enterprises were combined into units of more efficient size.

Many of the managers of the communal years were retained. Some managers were transferred from one enterprise to another, and a number moved into other pursuits. As need arose through expansion and the development of new enterprises, management talent was recruited from among the younger generation. Barlow reports that the various businesses were classified into groups for purposes of the monthly meetings. The meetings were held in Barlow's office except, in Barlow's words, "on real hot evenings in the summer when we held a few meetings outdoors on the lawn adjacent to my office."[22]

On April 10, 1932, the community kitchens were closed, and many Amana women found themselves with the task of preparing meals at home. With the help of Amana store managers, a sufficient number of kerosene stoves were found. The convenience of electricity was made available a few years later, in 1936. Many of the cooking utensils came from the community kitchens. The capitalistic problems of preparing economical meals in less than the large quantities of the community kitchens became a temporary problem. Although most families had taken food from the community kitchens to consume in their homes, closing the kitchens eliminated an important opportunity for social interaction. A significant reduction in the amount of food required in the Society occurred almost immediately. The amount of milk consumed was reduced by one-third and bread by one-half.[23] Under the communal system there was considerable waste because people took more free food than they could possibly use.

People were suddenly faced with the responsibility of providing for themselves and their families. As Rettig wrote, "Quite abruptly came the uncomfortable realization that he who would eat must work. So it was that many a 'sick' brother and sister miraculously regained his or her health during this period."[24] The adjustment was somewhat eased by permitting members to continue to live rent-free in their houses until January of 1933. After that they could purchase their homes at an appraised value, often through the sale of their distributive shares, or they could rent them at a relatively low rate. Groceries could be purchased for cost plus a small handling charge, and garden plots provided additional food. Some members still had credit at the stores, and others were given credit against future share sales or dividends.

The new corporation found that there were more job seekers than jobs. There were no work opportunities for the two hundred or more hired hands, and they were dismissed. Many other activities in which people had been employed before the Change could not be sustained economically. Some members were able to obtain employment in the surrounding towns and cities. A few people started small businesses of their own. With some exceptions, those who continued employment in the Society were paid a relatively low wage of ten cents an hour. Although the Society was not without assets, the lack of adequate cash flow made the policy necessary. It should be remembered that these were depression years, and the prices were correspondingly low. After the first year wages were raised to more realistic levels.

The large Amana agricultural and forestry enterprises were reorganized to gain the advantages of scale. Modern farm equipment and the latest scientific techniques were introduced. A great deal of attention was given to determining the best breed of cattle and hogs as well as the most productive agricultural crops. Farm managers were sent to Iowa State College for instruction in agronomy and animal husbandry.

The Change brought about major moves to develop modern infrastructure to support business enterprise and living standards. The Amana Society Telephone Company was formed a short time later. Another subsidiary corporation, Amana Woolens, Inc., was established to facilitate the marketing of Amana woolens.

Some existing business enterprises were strengthened and new ones were introduced. The rapid growth in the automobile population gave rise to two gasoline stations in Homestead and Amana, and somewhat later to one in South Amana, all of which were constructed in the architectural style of old Amana. A feed-milling operation was established in Homestead. A Society insurance agency was formed to provide life, fire, and other insurance. Bakeries and meat shops were consolidated and modernized.

A small business started shortly after the Change by George C. Foerstner of High Amana was to become a major nationally and internationally recognized enterprise.[25]

Foerstner studied the technology of refrigeration and, with Otto Zuber and Len Graf, built a beverage cooler. The handcraft of the cabinetmaker was involved; the outer shell was fir wood with beaded grooves, much like the wainscoting used on porch ceilings in the 1920s. Some of the early upright freezers had a wooden skeleton structure into which was fitted the cork insulation used at that time. The door frames were made of oak.

The company formed in 1932 by Foerstner with help from Arthur Barlow was the Amana Equipment Company. The name was changed a year later to the Electric Equipment Company. However, the use of the Amana name for private profit created difficulties with the Amana Society that were resolved through the purchase of the business by the Society. Foerstner continued as manager of what was then known as the Refrigeration Division, located for a time in Amana and then moved to Middle Amana, the present site of the business. The plant was rebuilt after a major fire in 1943, and a year later it became a million dollar business. In the late forties the Refrigeration Division built the first upright home freezer and, somewhat later, freezer-refrigerator combinations.

The rapid growth of the enterprise created major financial needs for further expansion. The Amana Society board felt that it lacked the expertise and resources for this purpose. In 1950 the decision was made to sell the business for $1,100,000 to Amana Refrigeration, Inc., a corporation founded by Foerstner; Howard Hall, an industrialist from Cedar Rapids; and several others. Under Foerstner's continued leadership the corporation rapidly expanded revenues and profits as it developed such new products as a compact room air-conditioner and a portable microwave oven. In 1965 Amana Refrigeration, Inc., became a subsidiary of the Raytheon Company. The fledgling enterprise of less than twenty employees in 1936 has a labor force today of more than three thousand in Middle Amana and in two locations in Tennessee.

The development of business enterprise in Amana gave rise to a controversy involving the use of land owned by the original Amana Society but conveyed to members who received title to these properties. A few of the business en-

Amana Refrigeration, Inc., 1953. (Photographic Collection, Amana Refrigeration, Inc.)

terprises on such land had expanded their original product lines beyond that considered proper by the Amana board of directors. For example, a business established as a winery was also selling packaged cheese and meat. The Iowa District Court granted an injunction restraining such actions on the grounds that these businesses had agreed to accept regulations of the Society board on land use and that a "general scheme" of land-use control existed.

Some of the directors were concerned that the growth of commercialism, and especially tourist-oriented businesses, was threatening the unique character of the Amana colonies, and they felt that restrictive measures should be adopted. They contended that land-use control was absolutely essential for this purpose. On the other side was the claim that the Society was far more interested in controlling competition for its own businesses than in land-use control. This conflict was divisive both within the Society and the board itself. Some of the defendants were members of the board and all were stockholders of the corporation suing them.

The case was appealed to the Iowa Supreme Court,

which reversed the district court and ruled that the defendants were protected by an Iowa law that prohibits "use restrictions" after twenty-one years unless such restrictions are refiled with the county recorder. The Society had failed to do so, which had the effect of negating any restrictions. The court further ruled that there was no "general scheme" of land-use control that could be used to restrict the property rights of the defendants.[26]

The ruling did not completely open the door to any business development. What it did was to permit far greater freedom in land use to persons who had purchased land from the original Society. Only those whose land had not been registered within the prescribed twenty-one years were affected. The difficulty was that this covered most of the private residential and business properties in the Amana Society. The Iowa Supreme Court decision almost immediately gave rise to new business establishments, essentially in the tourism area.

The Iowa Supreme Court noted that it had no alternative but to enforce the law and suggested that if the Amana colonies felt that the law was inappropriate, the case "should have been addressed to the legislature, not to this court."[27] The Society was quick to follow this path and gained the passage of legislation specifically designed for the Amana Society.[28] This legislation made possible the establishment of special land-use districts through the auspices of county government. It provided for hearings and elections to determine whether a land-use district is desired, and if so, the boundaries of such a district. If a district is established, an election is then held to select a seven-member board of trustees that has the power to develop land-use regulations with appropriate provisions for administration and enforcement.

This legislation addressed a concern expressed by the Iowa Supreme Court that since less than one-third of the residents of the colonies at that time were members of the Society, the franchise on such matters should not be restricted to only the members of the Society who vote for the board.[29] An Amana Colonies Land-Use District (ACLUD) has been established encompassing all of the villages except West Amana, which voted not to be included. In addition to

expanding the constituency for purposes of land-use control, what Amana is today has in a real sense been rede-
fined. This question will be given particular consideration
in Chapter 11.

The issue of land use affected the development of the
Amana furniture industry. Prior to the Change of 1932
there were three cabinet shops: one each in Amana, Middle
Amana, and East Amana. The board decided to continue
the shop in Amana to develop an expanded Society-owned
furniture enterprise. The Amana furniture industry subsequently prospered in a surge of development and entrepreneurship. In addition to the Society furniture shop, four privately owned enterprises presently make up this industry.
The restrictions on land use placed in the original deed con-
ferring Society-owned land to private individuals gave rise
to furniture enterprises a short distance from the original
Society boundaries. Two Amana cabinetmakers, Dave
Krauss and Norman Shantz, established sizable furniture
enterprises on outside private land between Homestead and
South Amana. A smaller shop operated by another cabinetmaker is located a short distance from Amana for the same
reason. A fourth furniture enterprise, located in West
Amana and owned by a cabinetmaker from Germany, benefited from the Iowa Supreme Court ruling and the vote of
West Amana not to be included in the special Amana land-
use district. None of the four private furniture enterprises is
permitted to use the trademark name of Amana. These enterprises and the Amana Furniture Shop, which can be cat-
egorized as the furniture industry of Amana, will be considered next.

CHAPTER 10

The Amana
Furniture Industry

At the time of the Change in 1932, there were three remaining cabinet shops: one each in Amana, Middle Amana, and East Amana. A cabinet shop in South Amana had been destroyed by fire in 1927. The shops in Amana and Middle Amana were the largest, with about the same amount of equipment. Prior to 1932 most of the furniture produced in the shops had been made for members and the Society. Occasionally a cabinetmaker would make a piece of furniture for a friend on the outside.

The Amana Furniture Shop

After the Change the new business manager of the Amana Society, Arthur Barlow, strongly encouraged board members to expand production of high-quality handcrafted furniture for a broader market. The board gave its approval and selected the cabinet shop in Amana to be the main cabinet shop. August Franke, the oldest cabinetmaker in Amana at that time, was given the managerial responsibility for developing the enterprise. The remaining cabinet shops were kept operational for a time to make minor pieces of furniture. The best of the basic equipment was moved to Amana, and a number of the most skilled cabinetmakers were employed in the Society-owned and -operated cabinet shop. Furniture for sale to the public was soon produced. At first business was slow, but it gradually expanded, and the enterprise became the Amana Furniture Shop.[1]

The early years were filled with adjustment, experimentation, determination, decision, and sometimes indecision. August Franke soon felt he was more interested in creating furniture than handling the financial and managerial aspects. As a result he was put in charge of the six cabinetmakers and all cabinetmaking, and John Noe became the manager of the business side. When Franke retired and Noe moved along to another enterprise, Jake Zscherny assumed responsibility for the technical and managerial functions of the organization. By June 1936,

Deacon's bench. This multiple-seating piece is a popular piece of furniture that is currently being handcrafted. The spindle back and simple turning tend to give it an Amana look. (Courtesy, Amana Furniture Shop)

twelve cabinetmakers were at the workbenches. (See Appendix C for a list of managers after 1932.)

The furniture first produced for outside customers was largely limited to the designs created and used by the Inspirationists through their years in America, primarily functional and utilitarian pieces that fulfilled the needs of a pioneering people. These pieces were characterized by straight lines, straight legs, simple turning, panel construction, and the absence of decoration. Sizes for pieces such as beds were not standard as they are today. On singular occasions there would be evidence of a strong German heritage and the kind of detail characteristic of the designs these people had known in Europe. The decision was made to try to gradually expand the business by broadening the choices available to include those currently popular in the world outside the Amanas.

What was the style of the day? Word of modish dress and current design in furniture did not travel fast to mid-America in the 1930s; the mail-order catalog and a few newspaper advertisements were probably the best communicators of the day. The homes in the small towns and rural areas of Iowa reflected influences of the Victorian period, Mission style, art nouveau, and "early attic." The then new Modern or "Moderne" style of the outer world included furniture forms that were somewhat lighter in appearance, simpler (had minor ornamentation), and more modest in scale and that maximized the character of the material used, such as the grain of wood. The eye level of the imaginary furniture line around the room gradually became lower, with the seats of chairs and table tops somewhat closer to the floor.

Much new furniture at the time, both in Europe and the larger population centers in the United States, was being made by mass production methods. Reproductions of some handcrafted pieces made decades earlier as well as current designs could be made more quickly and for less money. As these methods became more popular, the quality of design and materials decreased considerably. The copies of lesser quality became known as "Borax" furniture, after the cleaning agent that frequently gave premiums as "extra" value, and the finished products were quite different from the well-made, handcrafted furniture that had been cherished in the Amanas through many generations.[2]

The Society board members agreed it was essential that the high standard of workmanship and quality of Amana furniture remain the same as during earlier years. Amana handcrafted furniture would continue to be of heirloom quality. The new emphasis was to be on the development of more worldly and current designs in addition to the traditional Amana-inspired designs.

A portion of one of the buildings housing the present-day Amana Furniture Shop was part of the original Amana calico print mill built in 1857. In 1923 the mill was destroyed by a fire resulting from an explosion in the nearby flour mill; almost all of the eleven buildings were destroyed. The rebuilt area became the calico print factory, which operated until the dyes were no longer available in 1917. A section of this space was then diverted to cabinetmaking and eventually became the home of the present Amana Furniture Shop.

In the years following World War II the United States experienced new challenges and innovations that influenced the furniture industry. The Amana board became aware that major changes were needed if the local industry was to keep pace and be competitive. In 1958 a number of changes were made. The reorganization started with the appointment of Marvin Bendorf as the director of sales and marketing, who began with only a cigar box for cash and, as yet, no employees in the sales department. At the end of the first year Bendorf submitted a developmental plan that included the suggestion that more display areas be built and that a consultant be engaged to maximize workshop design. The plan was approved and the building was started in 1959 and completed in 1960. The display rooms provided a more effective way to show visitors the kinds of items that could be made. The changes and new facility also made possible greater space for the production of furniture since the original display room was now available for additional workbenches.

In 1967 a major expansion took place in the workshop production area. Again, with the help of a design and efficiency consultant, a new workshop was completed. This allowed for more workbenches and adequate space for the craftsmen. During the following ten years, four more expansions took place, including additions of a new finishing room, a warehouse, lumber storage areas, and a wood preparation area. These developments were justified by the dramatic growth in the demand for Amana-quality furniture. At present, visitors taking a shop tour can see part of the workshop where craftsmen demonstrate their skills in handcrafting solid wood furniture. A large part of the original workshop was converted to a display room for approximately 150 clocks.

The basic materials and techniques have remained the same; the processes have been refined. Amana Furniture Shop cabinetmakers continue to make furniture from solid walnut and solid cherry, woods native to the Amana area and probably two of the finest furniture woods grown anywhere. Unfortunately, the Amana board had been forced in the early post-1932 years to sell walnut logs to outsiders to help solve a critical cash flow problem. But until the 1940s and 1950s the Amana Society was able to fill the needs of the Amana Furniture Shop from the twelve thousand acres of Amana timberland, and to do it at a reasonable cost. Since then such woods have become scarcer locally and nationally and have greatly appreciated in value.

Today, the Amana Furniture Shop purchases most of the wood from the outside. On rare occasions a customer may want to supply his own wood for a desk or chair. Current supplies of walnut for furniture are grown primarily in seven midwestern states; much of the wild cherry or black cherry is grown in Appalachia. It takes sixty years for a walnut tree to become large enough to be cut for the making of furniture.

In the last few decades customer requests created an awareness of the need for a furniture hardwood that was more informal and casual to meet the requirements of changing life-styles. In response the Amana Furniture Shop started using solid oak and offering it in all of the pieces handcrafted there. This proved to be a sound decision as the demand for oak furniture has increased annually; at present, oak is requested for almost fifty percent of the customer orders.

Clock showroom. Many models of grandfather, grandmother, granddaughter, wall hanging, and shelf clocks can be seen and heard. (Courtesy, Amana Furniture Shop)

Skilled artisans cherish the warmth and quality that each of the hardwoods imparts; they can help customers choose a kind of wood and finish compatible with the form and function of the furniture piece to be made. Each of the woods has its own graining and other outstanding individual characteristics. The hand-applied, hand-rubbed finishes further enhance the beauty of the solid hardwoods.

As the wood arrives in the delivery area, it is the responsibility of one individual in the shop to inspect both sides of the boards; to cut the seasoned, kiln-dried lumber into predetermined lengths; and to place it in appropriate bins. The wood is planed to a uniform thickness. All pieces must be smooth and straight. When a project is set up, it is assigned a work number; that number is used on a particular piece throughout the production process. After the dimensions of the wood for the project have been specified, the lumber is matched according to grain, then boards are glued and put into a cart for the cabinetmaker at his workbench.

The cabinetmaker proceeds to create a new table or desk from start to finish that may take six or sixty hours to complete. An accurate account of the time spent for the construction of each piece is maintained. One exception to this procedure may be for those pieces that require turning—legs, bedposts, and spindles. In such instances another craftsman with the proper expertise completes this process on a hand-operated, wood-turning lathe, producing one component at a time. As in all handmade items, slight differences can be found in each of the parts, which add character to the finished product. As the cabinetmaker contours the materials to the exact and final shape, size, and design and starts to meticulously assemble the parts, he stamps the work number on the underside of the piece in an appropriate and inconspicuous spot. This number, along with other pertinent information, is recorded for reference in case the customer chooses to refer to it for additional matching or coordinating pieces of furniture in the future.

Two basic, age-old techniques for joining are used—techniques that were believed to have originated with the ancient Egyptians. One such technique is the dovetail, a joint where the angled and flaring extension of one piece of wood fits into the angled and flaring extension of a second piece to make a tight and secure piecing of the two sections. This type of joint is used in the construction of durable drawers. The second technique is the mortise-and-tenon joint, in which the end of one piece of wood is cut to fit into an opening in the end of a second piece. Such construction provides for a very strong joint. While these are done with the help of machines, the process is not automated and requires the skill of a cabinetmaker to produce a proper joint. These techniques make one-of-a-kind furniture possible.

A special quality of the furniture of Amana is the richness and warmth of the satiny smooth hand-rubbed finish. This finish accentuates the beauty of the natural wood and safeguards the integrity of the solid walnut, cherry, and oak. The Amana finishing process has evolved through generations of experience. Very little has changed in the finishing procedure; however, the materials available today are superior to those of former days, and consequently the Amana hand-rubbed finish is more durable and beautiful than ever before.

At the Amana Furniture Shop the finish is all brush applied. The cabinetmakers feel that the sealers and varnishes must be applied by brush to assure proper thickness and depth, allowing the hand-rubbing procedure to bring out the beauty of the natural woods. The finish color is determined early for made-to-order pieces. Some customers select the natural tones of the woods, while others want to match the color of pieces they already possess.

The first step in the finishing process is the application of the sealer, which prevents moisture from entering the

These women are highly skilled at executing the various steps in the finishing processes. Women are employed as finishers throughout the Amana furniture industry. (Courtesy, Amana Furniture Shop)

pores of the wood surface. The sealer is allowed to dry for approximately one day, then the surface is hand sanded in preparation for varnishing. Three to five coats of varnish are applied, depending on the nature of the piece, type of wear, and kinds of exposure it is expected to receive. There is a drying and waiting period between each application. The varnish is hand sanded lightly before each coat, and after the last coat has been applied, the finish is allowed to set up for several days to a hard consistency.

The final sanding and rubbing then begin. The process is completed with very fine steel wool and sandpaper to assure a smooth and soft touch. Great skill is required to assure that the sanding does not break through the various base coats that have been applied. This procedure is followed by gently wiping the surface with a paste made of rottenstone and oil. The paste has a slight polishing effect and leaves a soft, smooth, satiny finish with a richness and warmth that will last for generations.

The finishing procedure is completed by individuals other than the person who actually handcrafted the piece. It often requires up to two weeks to complete the finishing procedure. Before going to the customer or showroom, the furniture is stamped with a permanent Amana trademark and signed by the cabinetmaker—symbols of authenticity and the pride of the maker.

All the Amana furniture-making enterprises have a backlog of several months on custom orders, but they find that this does not create problems. Customers graciously accept this fact and are willing to wait as long as necessary, for they are waiting for an item of quality made particularly for them and their homes.

The amount of training and the degree of specialization vary with the individual cabinetmaker. A few have learned their skills from family or Society members, as was done in the past. Some began their careers as apprentices and advanced as they mastered skills and techniques. A few employed in the Amana Furniture Shop achieved their expertise by attending special schools. Others come to the shop as experienced artisans and can handle the most complex custom requirements. Women are especially adept at finish work. The Amana Furniture Shop presently employs about forty people in the workshop.

In the post-Change and postwar years innovation in the design of furniture was slow to appear; however, life-styles and housing designs were beginning to change. Ranch-style homes with reduced floor space and living room–dining room combinations became the answer to the housing shortage. They required furniture of different proportions and simple lines. For example, customers needed smaller dining tables, such as a drop-leaf table, that required less floor space when not in use but could be extended to seat twelve or fourteen people when needed. A few generations later as homes and dining rooms again became larger or separate and/or as family rooms were added, round and oval tables with extension features were introduced as standard pieces of furniture. These were adaptations of a basic table design that had been handcrafted in Amana for many generations.

Tourism grew in the 1960s. It soon became apparent that there was a need to offer additional designs that would appeal to a larger segment of the population. Between 1965 and 1980 about 150 new basic designs were introduced. Many were based on traditional designs, yet made to fit into a more contemporary setting. An example is the old-type spool cabinet with seven or eight shallow drawers; the inspiration for a new adaptation came from the designer seeing one in a farm home. The new version was similar in appearance, yet the number of actual drawers decreased while the storage space of the fewer drawers increased. This piece was made to serve as an end table.

The Amana Furniture Shop changed the specifications of rolltop desks in about 1975 when a customer brought to the attention of the manager that the partitions and storage sections of this style desk were no longer of proper size to be truly functional. Forms, stationery, and ledgers required new dimensions. Other items added about this time included doughbox end tables, large coffee tables, stereo and hi-fi cabinets, and wall sectional units that would accommodate television sets. Many of the pieces had only suggestions of traditional design, but there was no change in quality.

Designs are constantly being created or adjusted to fit

the needs of customers. A customer may want a wider or taller chair than is standard or need a piece to accommodate a particular space. One individual had vacationed in India near the Taj Mahal, where he purchased an eight-sided piece of white marble with subtle variegations. When he shipped it to the Amana Furniture Shop he knew he wanted to have a piece of furniture made that would incorporate the marble, but he didn't know what kind of piece he wanted. The manager, who also did much of the designing, and this customer decided to build an eight-sided cabinet with the marble on the top and a light on the interior to illuminate the cabinet top and dramatize the marble. Each of the side panels had an ogee arch suggestive of the upper curves of the slender minarets atop the Taj Mahal.

A prominent industrialist from Cedar Rapids needed wooden side chairs to complement a dining table. He wanted a type of spindle-back chair that had touches of traditionalism yet had clean-cut lines and that had a back somewhat lower than usual but with good proportions. The chair was designed and produced to his satisfaction, and he gave permission to use the design in making future chairs. Since that time many variations have been made for other customers, and they have become popular items. Within the organization, this chair informally has assumed the name of the customer; it also has a stamped number and the usual markings of identification.

The hanging wall clocks made by Frederick Hahn influenced the Amana furniture industry. His creations helped to establish a standard and design for clock production. The first floor models were made in 1940. In more recent years, many adaptations, sizes, and designs of wall, mantel, and floor-standing clocks have been added. Each clock cabinet is individually handcrafted by a skilled craftsman at a workbench, not produced en masse. The solid walnut and cherry cabinets house weight-driven movements purchased from Germany. The sale of Amana clocks currently makes up about twenty-five percent of the total business.

Customers appreciate the quality of Amana-made furniture, and some find great satisfaction in owning a piece that has been produced in a limited quantity rather

Lotus lily dry sink. This is a limited edition item. The rectangular pewter panels are pierced with a stylized version of the flower that blooms on the lake between Middle Amana and Amana. The wooden pulls on the drawer and doors are modified oak leaves. (Courtesy, Marvin and Emaline Bendorf)

than in great numbers. The Amana Furniture Shop successfully introduced a specified number of items in limited editions, including single furniture pieces and some clocks. The first was a small chest with two candle shelves, then the Ebenezer desk series, followed by the Amana lotus lily dry sink, a dry sink handcrafted in solid walnut and oak that incorporated hand-punched lily designs in its brass or pewter doors. After one year, the pattern and design of most limited edition items are destroyed.

One of the popular limited edition clock models is the Amana sandstone grandfather clock. This floor clock stands approximately seven feet tall, has hand carving in the crown, and has a special movement and dial design that make it a unique item. The paintings on the moon dial are based on two original oil paintings commissioned by a local artist, Ruth Schmieder. A total of 250 clocks will be handcrafted, then the pattern will be destroyed. It is estimated that it will take five years to produce this many clocks.

In 1979 the decision was made at the Amana Furniture Shop to include a copy of a Hahn-designed clock with the limited edition items. An original was taken to the workshop, where precise cabinet details were recorded for the process of duplication. Since Frederick Hahn had also made the movements, it was important to find someone who could make identical movements, if possible. The head clock technician took exact drawings to Germany to search for someone who could duplicate the movements. He found such a person in the Black Forest area of Germany. Since then, limited editions of the Hahn clock have been produced, with ninety-nine models crafted each year.

A third clock was the Engelthal bracket clock, which was named after the cloister in Germany near the Ronneburg that had been occupied for a time by some of the Inspirationists. *Engelthal* means "Angels Valley" and is descriptive of the serene Hessen valley where the cloister was located. This sixteen-inch-high design has a German triple chime that sounds every quarter hour; the walnut cabinet is embellished with an engraved plaque identifying it as a limited edition.

Another clock in the group that exemplifies the importance of the Amana people's German background is the Ysenburg model. This clock was made to give recognition to the Ronneburg Castle, the early home of many Inspirationists, and the Ysenburg family, who still own the castle and various adjacent properties. Early in 1983 the sales manager made drawings for a wall clock that had triple chimes and a hand-carved crown. Upon completion the clock was carefully crated and shipped to Germany.

The plan included a presentation by Marvin Bendorf, the manager of the Amana Furniture Shop, to Prince Ysenburg in a special ceremony. Even though the clock had been shipped several weeks in advance and with the essential safeguards, the day before the ceremony the clock could not be found. By coincidence, the prince's youngest son was soon to be married; the person in charge of affairs had assumed that this beautiful clock from the United States was a wedding present. It was delivered and put in place at the groom's new home. At the time Prince Ysenburg was traveling in Spain and was unaware of what had happened.

While the clock was being duly moved from the groom's home and readied for the ceremony, Bendorf was preparing the text of his presentation, which was to be delivered in both German and English. Bendorf was faced with a difficult question. How should the prince be respectfully addressed? The words *Eure Durchlaucht* (Your Serene Highness) were selected. On August 21, 1983, Bendorf personally presented the first Ysenburg model to the prince and his family in a formal ceremony at the Ronneburg *Schloss* in Hesse.

The following year the prince came to the Amanas, at which time he visited the Amana Furniture Shop and autographed twenty-five of the clocks. A total of fifty clocks are handcrafted every year, and each is identified with a numbered brass plate designating the position of that particular clock in the production sequence.

Later the Amana Heritage Collection was added. This special group of items consists of reproductions of small useful accessory items found in old Amana homes and thus serves as an additional link to the past. The collection includes such items as silverware trays, decorative shelves, spoon holders, small corner shelves, traditional Amana coat and hat racks, salt boxes, and candlesticks. All pieces are signed by the maker. The Amana Furniture Shop also has a commercial sales department that handles business gift and accessory items such as desk clocks, bookends, pencil holders, and boxes.

The Amana Furniture Shop has added several supplementary lines. In 1979 the manager visited Germany to search for high-quality cuckoo clocks. At that time a relationship was developed with several makers of cuckoo clocks in the Black Forest region who are currently supplying quality cuckoo clocks to the Amana Furniture Shop. These clocks have become a high volume item.

In addition, a few lines of non-Amana furniture have been added and are available for purchase. As Bendorf commented, "This gives a customer a wider selection." All Amana handcrafted pieces in the shop are ticketed with "Amana Blue" tickets; items made outside Amana have beige hang tags naming the company that produced the item. Bendorf stated that "these additions have in no way diminished the production and availability of Amana-made pieces since that portion of the business has increased."

Marvin Bendorf made a number of important contributions to the Amana furniture industry. He played a major role in applying advanced management and marketing techniques in the Amana Furniture Shop. The product line and mix were adapted to changing economic and market conditions. Workshop and showroom spaces were enlarged and modernized. Advertising and other sales promotions were utilized to expand the market area. A number of external marketing outlets were established. Computerized and electronic informational systems helped promote more efficient business operations.

The new manager, David Rettig, is well qualified to continue the progress made by Bendorf. His baccalaureate degree from the University of Iowa and extensive managerial experience in other Amana enterprises will serve him well. Rettig plans to give further emphasis to the enlargement of the market for Amana furniture. He comes from an old and distinguished Amana family; his great-great-grandfather was the well-known Amana clockmaker, Frederick Hahn.

The Amana Furniture Shop was the first furniture enterprise in what was to become an Amana furniture industry. By 1956 an Amana Furniture Shop manager and cabinetmaker, Dave Krauss, launched his privately owned furniture-making business, the Krauss Furniture and Clock Factory. Ten years later, in 1966, one of the Krauss cabinetmakers, Norman Schanz, created another privately owned business, the Schanz Furniture and Refinishing Shop. Dean

Berger, in Amana, and Walter Kraft, in West Amana, have smaller specialized operations.

The three large enterprises and two smaller ones make up a sizable Amana furniture industry. The procedures involved in the construction and finishing of furniture are based on time-tried traditions and are basically the same throughout the Amana area. Each, however, has its own refinements.

Krauss Furniture and Clock Factory

The Krauss Furniture and Clock Factory was started in 1956 by Dave Krauss, his daughter Virginia, and his son Marvin. Their ancestors arrived in Amana in 1867 from Germany and Ebenezer, and they settled in South Amana. Cabinetmaking has played a role in this family through five generations. Dave Krauss was the manager of the Society-owned Amana Furniture Shop from 1951 to 1956.

At the time the new firm was established, the Amana Society required privately owned businesses to be built on privately owned land. Krauss purchased two acres from the Roy Hunzelman family, whose holdings included a strip of land one-half mile east of South Amana that extended from the Iowa River south to what is now U.S. Highway 6.

The business was opened in a new building that measured approximately forty-one feet by one hundred feet. While most of the tools and equipment used by a cabinetmaker are standard, Krauss started with mostly used items, some of which have been rebuilt and are still in use.

Six people were employed. All were individuals the Krauss family knew personally, and all lived within the perimeters of Amana. Virginia assumed the bookkeeping duties, while Dave and Marvin were involved directly with making furniture. Everyone worked a minimum of eight hours a day; a nine-hour day was not unusual. Employees had no complaints about a forty- to fifty-hour work week. The only perk was a one- or two-week paid vacation.

Today the Krauss Furniture and Clock Factory occupies a much-expanded facility of approximately twenty thousand square feet, including a reception area, four large

Work area in a cabinet shop. Workbenches of the cabinetmakers line the exterior wall. (Courtesy, Krauss Furniture and Clock Factory)

showrooms, office spaces, a large construction area, a finishing room, and several areas for storing lumber. What seems like hundreds of tracing patterns for arcs and curves of all sizes are hung on nails and hooks around the walls of the work area. Additional state-of-the-art equipment has been added as needed and as the enlargement of space allowed. The number of employees has increased to twenty-five, with ten cabinetmakers and two individuals handling sales and records. Dave Krauss passed away in 1965; Marvin became the manager and Virginia the secretary-treasurer.

In contrast to earlier days, employees have up to three weeks of vacation, six or seven paid holidays, and medical insurance. Vacation may be taken at any reasonable time the employee chooses, and the work load is adjusted accordingly. All the individuals working in the cabinet shop

are skilled cabinetmakers who developed their expertise
working with wood under the guidance of a father or other
relative; none has come from special woodworking schools.
Turnover is almost nonexistent; therefore, on-the-job training in the "Krauss tradition" is of minimal concern. Employees are dedicated, hardworking, and pleased with their
working conditions. They stay with the organization. In the
rare instance when a replacement is needed or an artisan
must be added, the cabinetmaker with mechanical aptitude
and abilities would likely be given high priority. (All cabinetmakers here are men.)

The new cabinetmaker would be started on one process

*Cabinetmaker perfecting a table leg on a lathe. The tools on the
short wall above are used to measure the precise circumference of
pieces being turned. (Courtesy, Krauss Furniture and Clock Factory)*

or one kind of furniture that was relatively easy to make. He would be kept on that kind of work for an orientation period of six to eight months. His assignments would be gradually expanded until he had sufficient expertise to meet the required standards. He would then be given a more specialized type of construction, such as the making of case pieces. Basically, each piece of Krauss furniture is handcrafted by one cabinetmaker. From time to time a person may be shifted to another piece if need arises.

Each cabinetmaker has his own workbench, with tools provided by Krauss. Traditional hand processes as practiced in the past are still used; some modern mechanized equipment helps refine the processes. There is undoubtedly some feeling of competition among the artisans, but the goal is an end product of highest quality. Some cabinetmakers work fast; others work more painstakingly. Pay is determined by the amount of quality production by the individual worker.

Women have been employed in this firm since 1956; they have a special aptitude for executing the finishing processes and enjoy the work. Krauss cabinetmakers, as well as other cabinetmakers employed in the Amana area, are not members of a craft guild or similar organization.

The Krauss Furniture and Clock Factory uses mostly walnut, cherry, and oak, with at least ninety percent of all the wood ordered from outside the Amana area. The lumber arrives by truck. Wood shavings and sawdust cover the floor of the workshop in considerable abundance. Both of these biodegradable materials are disposed of in a manner similar to that used in the past—blowing them outside into a mound through a twelve-inch metal pipe. Farmers are given all they need for bedding of turkeys, horses, and cattle.

While the materials and techniques remain basically the same, glue has changed. In the late 1880s and early 1900s glue was purchased in sheets and pieces from a nearby meat processing plant. The dry glue was soaked overnight in water, then heated in a large double-boiler-like copper kettle. Later, glue became available in powdered form, which shortened the soaking time. Today, the same quality of glue is used, but it is a synthetic product.

Only a natural finish is applied to solid walnut or cherry wood. Age and light tend to alter the final color, with cherry becoming slightly darker and walnut lighter.

In addition to chests, tables, chairs, high chairs, rockers, beds, footstools, desks, whatnots, bookcases, hutches, carts, washstands, and numerous other furniture pieces, production of floor clocks, wall clocks, and tabletop clocks are an important segment of the business. There are tall and impressive grandfather clocks; a somewhat smaller clock called the grandmother clock; and a newcomer to the family of clocks, the granddaughter clock. After World War II Dave Krauss started to make clocks in the basement of his home as a hobby. His skill and reputation as a clockmaker developed rapidly. He built his first clock for retail sale in 1956. Since then many types and styles of residential clocks have been and presently are being built in the Krauss factory.

A number of the Krauss clocks have many similarities to the clocks made by Frederick Hahn. The precision-timed movements and a majority of the faces are purchased from Germany; the remainder of the faces are obtained from sources in the United States. The Krauss-designed cabinets are handcrafted from walnut, cherry, and oak. Most of the floor clocks are weight-driven, one-week clocks. The soft melodic chimes of any particular clock are of two types: a single chime, which is the Westminster chime (it plays a Westminster tune); or a triple or three-chime, which is composed of the Whittington chime, Saint Michael chime, and Westminster chime. The showroom clocks are set on different time schedules so that the harmonious, bell-like tones can be heard almost continuously from the time one enters the front door.

Krauss customers may choose from a broad selection of Krauss-designed and handcrafted furniture on display in the several salesrooms. An experienced cabinetmaker has the touch for making such pieces without many drawings or other written specifications. To be more cost-efficient, these pieces are often built in pairs.

Customers also have the option of having furniture made from their own designs, dimensions, and wood. For such individual pieces, measured drawings are made, and

Classic Amana rocker. Every Amana living room had a rocker built in this basic, traditional style. (Courtesy, Krauss Furniture and Clock Factory)

the customer approves all details of the plans before the work begins. Entertainment centers, computer furniture, and units to accommodate a wall of books in a home library have been popular items. Clients may bring their own wood if it is of proper quality and sufficient in quantity to complete a project. In the case of walnut, the wood a customer would bring in is likely to be unsteamed and redder in color because the wood needs to be treated almost immediately after the tree is cut to blend the sap. The commercially prepared wood arrives at the factory steamed and somewhat different in appearance.

There is approximately a ten-month waiting period for custom-made furniture to be completed. The Krauss Furniture and Clock Factory guarantee is that every piece of furniture must be satisfactory to the customer; if anything is wrong a correction or a replacement will be made.

In addition to the custom orders and the standard furniture line offered by Krauss, some unique pieces can be seen in the showroom. One example is the Becky Lee table, a reproduction of a southern plantation table that has curvaceous supports. The story accompanying the design of the table is that an old gentleman of the South had a table de-

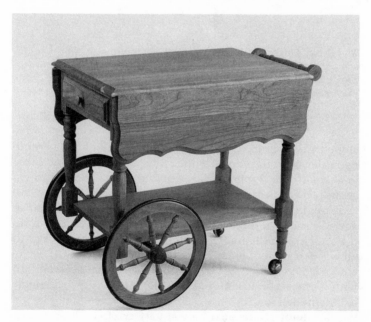

Cherry tea cart. This has been a popular handcrafted item for homes with a traditional look. (Courtesy, Krauss Furniture and Clock Factory)

The Becky Lee table. This table was originally made for a southern gentleman who specified "many curvilinear lines." It is currently being handcrafted. (Courtesy, Krauss Furniture and Clock Factory)

signed and built in this manner to remind him of his granddaughter, who had no straight lines. Another unique piece is a small side table with several kinds of locally grown grain placed under a glass top. This specialty piece is one that might be of particular interest to people involved in agriculture, or it might serve as a souvenir to visitors from distant lands. Still another unique item is a floor clock with all wooden components. This unusual clock—a one-day, no-chime clock—is five feet tall and has a one-meter pendulum with a one-second tick; it is built for Krauss by an outside cabinetmaker.

The showrooms also have a variety of small accessory items that have been made by skilled craftsmen who are retired or otherwise employed. The items include salad bowls, wooden lamp bases, thimble boxes, trivets, trays, and music boxes. They also sell the powdered furniture glue, accompanied by a "quick and easy" recipe, as a base for coloring Easter eggs.

The Krauss Furniture and Clock Factory does minimal advertising. A great many of the potential customers know the reputation of Amana-made quality products. Repeat business is excellent. A number of pieces of bedroom furniture in the official mansion of the governor of Iowa were made by this firm.

An independent and well-written quarterly publication titled *Willkommen* carries small advertisements for local businesses, both private and Society-owned. The Amana

Four-poster headboard. This is an example of a walnut handcrafted item that may be purchased from the showroom. Made-to-order pieces from all the cabinet shops are likely to require a waiting period of many months. (Courtesy, Krauss Furniture and Clock Factory)

Travel Council prepares general information for the tourist. Businesses share the cost. Furniture and clocks are sold nationwide directly (with no distributors); the greatest concentration of sales is in Iowa and the surrounding states.

Marvin Krauss expressed his feelings about his work, his business enterprise, and his outlook on life by saying, "The cabinet shop is always a happy place to work."

Schanz Furniture and Refinishing Shop

In true and typical Amana tradition, the Schanz Furniture and Refinishing Shop in South Amana is built on the expertise, dedication, hard work, and pride of several generations of Schanz family members who were either cabinetmakers or were associated with the business, including great-grandfather Johannus, grandfather George, father Harry, his son Norman, and Norman's wife Joanna. Norman and Joanna are the present owners and managers. The established way of life may well be carried on to the next generation in that Norman's son Michael started working in the shop at age twelve; although he is currently attending a university, he might be associated with the business in the future. A daughter, who is now married and living elsewhere, spent many, many hours sanding furniture and working in sales and has a great appreciation for fine woods and handcrafted furniture.

Norman Schanz began his career working for Marvin Krauss of the Krauss Furniture and Clock Factory. His years there were productive and pleasant; however, his entrepreneurial instincts led him to want to do more. He started to refinish furniture in the basement of his home in West Amana in the evenings and on weekends. As soon as he could comfortably afford to do so, he had the dirt floor cemented and the work space and equipment upgraded.

One of his early jobs was for a customer who wanted him to restore an old drop-leaf table that had been used for multiple purposes and was in poor condition. On close examination it appeared that over eighty percent of the table needed more than repair and refinishing; the deteriorated wood would have to be replaced and thus the table would qualify as a new piece of furniture rather than a refinished piece. The customer also indicated that he might want four new chairs to match the table. This was cause for possible future problems in that the Schanz house was located on property owned by Schanz but controlled by Society deeds of earlier years. According to regulations then in effect he could not operate his own private business on the land and be a competitor of the Amana Society-owned and -operated Amana Furniture Shop.

This problem with the Society became more critical as the demand for Schanz's refinishing skills grew. It is the tradition of Amana and German people that whenever an item such as a piece of furniture is handed down from one generation to another, it is handed down in the best possible condition. For example, Fred Reudy had a *Schrank* and a captain's chair that needed refinishing before they were to be passed along to his children. He asked Schanz to do the work. These projects were followed by numerous other pieces of fine old furniture that Reudy wanted to give to family members. Friends and neighbors had similar needs, and Schanz was the only cabinetmaker refinishing furniture at that time. He soon found himself too busy to fulfill the responsibilities of a full-time job and do the extra work evenings and weekends.

In 1966 Schanz told Krauss, his employer, that he felt he needed to leave and establish his own organization. Krauss generously and kindly told Schanz, "If it doesn't work out for you, you can come back to the Krauss Furniture and Clock Factory to work. The bench is always open."

Norman and Joanna Schanz purchased land east of West Amana and constructed a building for their refinishing and related businesses. During these early years of developing the business, Joanna Schanz was gaining expertise and knowledge about the crafts of broom making and basket weaving. In 1971 the Schanzes built the Broom and Basket Shop adjacent to their refinishing facility. It was constructed in the style of typical Amana architecture, with a gabled roof, a covered porch, and trellises for grapevines. Antique outdoor furniture and artifacts, authentic cultured willow for baskets, and a background of green hills and timberland can be seen from the roadside. Among the interest-

ing brooms and baskets inside the shop is an old Amana-
made, foot-powered broom machine that was used in the
Amanas for a number of generations.

The building was originally planned for the making of
brooms—a craft handed down to Joanna from a blind
broom maker, Philipp Griess. In 1977 Joanna added basket
weaving, a craft she learned from Philip Dickel, the last active basket maker from old Amana. Her tutelage included
planting willow slips, harvesting and sorting the willow,
and learning the techniques involved in basket making.

Basket making had been a popular activity among the
Inspirationists since the days when the group had lived in
Hesse. The church Elders appointed a basket maker for
each village, usually an older person who was not as physically active as farm workers and others. Baskets of all
descriptions were used in daily life for carrying garden produce and grain, harvesting apples, transporting laundry
and clothes pins, holding bread dough while it was rising,
and keeping needles and yarns together for knitting.

The Schanzes own and operate the Broom and Basket
Shop as a private enterprise. Three full-time employees
make up the sales force. In addition to successfully operating a growing business, Joanna Schanz teaches basketry
classes and gives lectures and demonstrations throughout
the United States. She has won numerous competitions and
has written a book on the subject.

The largest facility presently owned and operated by
the Schanzes is the Schanz Furniture and Refinishing Shop
one-half mile east of South Amana on U.S. Highway 6. The
primary building stands on private land that was originally
owned by the Hunzelman family. A portion of this land was
sold to Ott Fisher of Algona, Iowa, who erected a building to
house an antique car museum. Fisher developed other interests and sold the large building to Schanz in 1979. It was
a welcome addition of space for both production and sales.
The structure immediately to the east was owned by the
Brumwell brothers of Solon and used as an outlet for
Brumwell flour and food products before Schanz bought it.

The Schanz Furniture and Refinishing Shop is spa-
cious. Two large salesrooms are filled with a seemingly endless variety of beautiful handcrafted tables, chairs, beds,

Gateleg table. An adaptation of an old table style, it is compatible with many kinds of current interior decor. Square, tapered legs can be found on many pieces of Amana furniture. (Courtesy, Schanz Furniture and Refinishing Shop)

chests, washstands, dry sinks, whatnots, desks, bookcases, and much, much more. Schanz-made unfinished furniture and Schanz-brand sealers and varnishes are for sale. The hungry customer can select an assortment of food products with an Amana identity from horseradish to honey and jam to jelly as well as the Brumwell line of flours, oat bran, and pancake mixes. The space that was once used for grinding grain and making flour now provides a place for storing lumber and making picture frames. A huge supply of cut logs is stored at the rear of the main building for aging and drying.

In addition the Schanzes have a sales outlet in Amana, the Broom and Basket Shop and Furniture Outlet, which is housed in a building that was formerly a bakery. This store offers a nice variety of small gift and accessory items made of wood and a large selection of baskets crafted in the Schanz Broom and Basket Shop in West Amana.

Rocker components. Pieces for traditional Amana rockers are in the foreground. Note the pattern sticks hung at the top of the back wall above a workbench. (Courtesy, Schanz Furniture and Refinishing Shop)

The men and women employed at the Schanz Furniture and Refinishing Shop think of their work and skills as lifework. There is little turnover among the twelve cabinetmakers, who range in age from thirty-five to eighty. No special training manuals or orientation classes are needed here! Cabinetmakers have their own workbenches; tools are furnished by the firm. Cabinetmakers take care of their own quality control.

A noticeable difference from the other two cabinet shops is the way work assignments are given. The Amana Furniture Shop assigns one cabinetmaker to follow all the way through construction of one piece of furniture except for processes such as turning legs. The Krauss Furniture and Clock Factory basically assigns one cabinetmaker to a piece of furniture until it is finished, but does allow for some flexibility and shifting according to orders and needs of the day. Schanz gives approximately six jobs to a cabinet-maker, with a different kind of activity each day of the week, to relieve any possible monotony or boredom on the job. In each case the managers have stressed that their employees seem happy with their work schedules and that production is satisfactory.

Schanz uses a variety of woods—walnut, cherry, oak, hard maple, ash, hickory, and butternut. Other kinds of wood are used if customers request them. All wood used for furniture is seven-eighths-inch thick finished and of first and select (FAS) quality. In addition, logs of sometimes as much as 100,000 board feet are dried and cured for a four-to five-year period. This wood is used in "log run;" that is, the good wood and that of a little lesser quality are used together for small gift items such as key holders. Wood losses run about twenty-five percent in end pieces; however, pieces as small as four inches by four inches are utilized in the making of animal cutouts. Scraps are used as fuel in the wood-burning furnaces to heat the buildings. No wood is purchased from the Amana Society.

Construction techniques are much the same as they were generations earlier—they are all done in the old Amana way. Much panel construction is found on the ends of case pieces such as chests. Drawers are skillfully made with dovetail joints, without center guides, and with a flush fit. Mortise-and-tenon joints can be found in support areas where a strong joining of components is needed. The handcrafted pieces are signed and dated by the cabinet-maker.

Finishing is a time-consuming process that involves much sanding and the application of a four-coat, hand-rubbed finish. Schanz uses Schanz-brand sealers and varnishes, which he also sells to do-it-yourselfers. Schanz has no requests for painted or lacquered furniture.

Stock items are available from the floor or can be selected for construction from an illustrated brochure, a primary advertising tool. Considerable sales result from satisfied customers; it is rather common for customers to order additional furniture at the time they come to pick up a new heirloom. Custom orders make up about fifty percent of all

Recaning the back of an old side chair. To renew the chair, natural bamboo cane is used in the seven-step pattern. (Courtesy, Schanz Furniture and Refinishing Shop)

new orders, and customers may designate a choice of design, wood, finish, and dimensions for special orders. The cost does not vary with the kind of wood to be used. Larger orders are crated and shipped by a commercial van line. Out of deference to his neighbor, competitor, former employer, and friend Marvin Krauss, Schanz does not make or sell clocks.

A historically significant project executed by Schanz Furniture and Refinishing Shop was the creation of twenty-six walnut desk and chair reproductions of 1839 originals that were to be part of the permanent display in the House chamber of the Old Capitol in Iowa City, Iowa. The furniture was in place for the 1977 official reopening of Iowa's restored first capitol. Among others, Walter Kraft, whose work is described in the following section, helped with the handcrafting. The contract was made on a bidding basis.

In the Broom and Basket Shop in West Amana a visitor

can see what is probably Iowa's largest solid walnut rocker. The rocker was built on a three-to-one scale to a regular Amana rocker. It weights 670 pounds, is eleven feet tall, and contains around three hundred square feet of solid walnut wood; it required seventy-five hours to build and eleven hours to sand and finish. Schanz challenged his wife Joanna to cane the chair; she accepted. The caning took forty-eight hours. A coordinated footstool with an uphol-stered top accompanies the rocker.

The Schanz Furniture and Refinishing Shop is the only one that makes the traditional Amana lawn gliders, garden seats, and martin houses. Another unique item in the sales-room is a six-inch-long wooden whistle that emits the sounds of a steam train, a nostalgic sound to many a grand-parent who succumbs to buying the whistle for a grand-child.

A martin house currently built in Amana. For generations the Amana people have placed the birdhouses on high poles in their yards as havens for the birds. (Courtesy, Schanz Furniture and Refinishing Shop)

Wooten desk. A patent was granted to W. S. Wooten for this style desk on October 4, 1874. The approximate dimensions of the reproduction are seventy-two inches by forty-four inches by thirty inches. (Courtesy, Schanz Furniture and Refinishing Shop)

The jewel of the showroom in South Amana is a copy of a magnificent Wooten desk. The Wooten Desk Company was organized in 1874 and shortly afterward advertised the patented Wooten secretary. John D. Rockefeller, Jay Gould, Ulysses S. Grant, Joseph Pulitzer, and Charles Scribner were among the owners of originals. The Wooten desk was of the finest quality and exemplified the "post Civil-War mania for efficiency, order, and gadgetry." It was "a desk that rolled, locked, rotated, and whose writing flap dropped, letter flap snapped, an important innovation in America. In an era when one man with one large desk could operate a large business himself and keep all his records in one file, Wooten

Wooten desk, interior. This copy, made by an Amana cabinet-maker, is of solid walnut with Carpathian elm burl. The doors are dovetailed, the wood is finished with a four-coat, hand-rubbed finish, and the brass is of European style. (Courtesy, Schanz Furniture and Refinishing Shop)

brought the business man out of the era of keeping his records in the lining of his beaver hat and helped him cope with the ever increasing paper work of the Industrial Revolution."[3] The desk in the Schanz showroom was handcrafted by Schanz's cabinetmaker, Alan Trumpold; it required seventy-five hours of labor.

Kraft Furniture Shop

Amana was attractive to German-born immigrants, both Inspirationists and non-Inspirationists. Most of the non-Inspirationists came more directly to the Iowa frontier for reasons similar to those of many early settlers and were drawn to the Amanas for reasons of culture and language. Many became members of the Society; others stayed only until they had gained some economic independence and were able to establish themselves on the outside, often near the Amana lands.

The story of one highly successful cabinetmaker is similar in many respects. Walter Kraft, the son of a Lutheran minister in Germany, finished grade school at the end of World War II in Ichenheim on the Rhine at a time when the necessities of life were scarce. His father suggested that he apprentice with a cabinetmaker friend who had just returned from military service, even though Walter seemed to have an interest and aptitude for mechanics. Within a few years he was a journeyman cabinetmaker. He also learned construction techniques necessary for building residential housing. The father was hopeful that this younger son would also attend a university, as had his older brother who became an architect. Walter was happy in his work and felt that his years learning to work with wood should not be wasted.

He soon sought to expand his horizons. He moved to Switzerland, then to Canada, and in 1956 to Charles City, Iowa, to the home of his wife's parents. At that time housing needs in many communities were great, and Kraft built several apartment buildings in the area. He was pleased with his accomplishments in residential building but maintained a strong interest in cabinetmaking.

A made-to-order three-drawer walnut low chest with design influences characteristic of the Queen Anne period—curved lines,
cabriole legs, pad feet, walnut wood, inlay, and crossbanding. An
example of a piece that can be specified and made in Amana even
though it does not follow traditional Amana design. (Courtesy,
Kraft Furniture Shop)

Detail of the white
birch inlay on the
end panel of the
Queen Anne chest.
(Courtesy, Kraft Fur-
niture Shop)

The marketing of oneself as a cabinetmaker in the United States is quite different from such marketing in Germany. However, in a very short time he found himself with three excellent offers: one was outside Iowa, one was in a large city, and one was in Amana. The decision was not easy, but Amana was the winner.

Walter Kraft started working for the Amana Furniture Shop in October 1970 and remained there as a cabinetmaker until 1976. Subsequently, the Schanz Furniture and Refinishing Shop received a contract for making twenty-six walnut desk and chair reproductions of 1839 originals to be displayed in the House chamber of the Old Capitol in Iowa City, Iowa, the first capitol building for the state of Iowa. Kraft built the desks and helped with the making of other furniture parts. His wife, Erika, did much of the finish work. These outstanding pieces of handcrafted, hand-finished walnut furniture, complete with quill pens, provide the ambience befitting a chamber of that generation.

Today Walter Kraft privately owns the Kraft Furniture Shop and works as an individual cabinetmaker. He makes his own designs for the furniture he creates or builds to the requirements of a customer. Most of his items are one-of-a-kind, such as ladies' desks, credenzas, coffee tables, tambour-top desks, drop-leaf tables, and bedroom furniture. One special technique he uses is that of inlay, often referred to as marquetry, where a decorative pattern is created by cutting and inserting a design of contrasting wood into a form of the same shape on the basic surface. The tops of occasional tables, headboards, and the points of locks are enhanced with this intricate technique. Matching inlaid motifs may be found in the splats of dining room chairs, on the centers of dining room tables, or in the backs of Queen Anne chairs, which are likely to be slightly concave at shoulder level. Burled woods are frequently used for table tops or panels. His furniture has a look of distinction.

Kraft does no advertising, and his home-shop in West Amana is not located where a tourist is likely to browse. His business is almost entirely by word of mouth, yet his furniture can be found in homes in Chicago, Minneapolis, California, and the Carolinas. A customer may wait two years for an order to be completed, and the waiting list is long.

A son, Rudy, is following German tradition and the footsteps of his father; he has worked as a cabinetmaker for Krauss Furniture and Clock Factory for ten years. The Kraft family has gained from the development of the Amana furniture industry, which has in turn benefited from the special abilities and techniques of this family of skilled craftsmen.

The Berger Family: A Family of Artisans

Throughout Amana history many individuals have expressed their creative talent and craftsmanship by making furniture, toys, and other items of wood on a part-time basis or as a hobby. Such contributions have continued to this day and should be included in the Amana furniture enterprise. The Berger family has produced more than its share of such craftsmen.

Herman J. Berger and Mary Setzer Berger, the parents, were born in Amana during the early years of the settlement. As a young man, Herman was assigned by the Elders to work in the large farming operation of the Society, where he gained much knowledge about farm machinery and growing crops and trees. In time he became a farm manager, and this was his life's work. Herman and Mary were the parents of three sons: Fred, Dan, and Adolph (usually called A. T.). One son recalls that the family had a great love for the outdoors, and a favorite Sunday afternoon activity was a walk in the woods where they might spend some time identifying the plants and trees.

As a baby the eldest son, Fred, seemed to be attracted to mechanical devices. Before he could walk he showed an unusually great interest in the circular action of moving belts and wheels and the motion of the rotating parts of a machine caused by the forward thrust of a shaft. The fascination was such that he would often excitedly imitate such movement with his forearms when he saw machinery in operation. He particularly liked to watch the crews operate thrashing machines. During his adult life he became a self-taught machinist and could craft almost any piece of mechanical equipment needed. As a hobby when he was eighteen, he built many pieces of household furniture from available woods (especially ash) with tools and equipment he had made. His son, Dean, became skillful in woodcrafting; Dean owns the Berger Custom Woodwork Shop and still uses equipment and tools made by his father.

The second son, Dan, frequently stopped by the cabinet shop in his home village, South Amana, for an hour or so and helped with any tasks that an interested and adept thirteen- or fourteen-year-old could manage. After graduating from school Dan was assigned to work in the cabinet shop in South Amana. He liked his assignment, but after a few years felt he needed to take a look at the outside and went to Chicago to work.

Life in Amana was more to Dan's liking. He returned to Amana, the home village of his wife, a descendant of Joseph Prestele. He worked in the local garage for two years, then opened a gas station in Amana, where he spent thirteen years. After these varied work experiences, he knew his vocational future was to be one associated with cabinetmaking and the furniture industry. A fortunate sequence of events led to his taking the position of general manager of the Amana Furniture Shop. Within a few years he decided he would rather oversee actual furniture making at the workbenches than to manage the business operation in an office.

Dan was an expert craftsman and was highly respected for his abilities. He enjoyed the challenges offered in unusual and more difficult types of construction techniques, such as creating tambour tops for rolltop desks and such pieces. In later years he moved to another Society-owned and -operated business that involved constructing case furniture for kitchens and businesses, various types of millwork, and special commercial installations.

A. T. Berger, the third son, has played an important role in the direction of both academic and leisure activity of children. His vocation was that of teacher; one of his hobbies was that of toy maker.

When he was fourteen the Elders determined he should become a teacher. Since the Iowa County town of Williamsburg was only ten miles from his home in South Amana and train service between the two communities was available, he traveled to and from Williamsburg weekly for four years to earn his high school diploma and a teaching certificate. He taught school for twenty-five years. Later he became a rural mail carrier for the U.S. Post Office and was a member of the committee of forty-seven, the group of leaders chosen to guide the Community of True Inspiration through the 1932 change from communism to capitalism. This talented and versatile man also writes poetry occasionally.

During his early years, woodworking was an avocation; in later years it played a much more important role. His workshop and display areas can be found in the building that once housed a restaurant and a thirteen-room hotel in Upper South, adjacent to the railroad. The hotel was the home away from home for traveling salesmen and people on vacation. Rooms that once were furnished with beds that had knotted ropes to support mattresses and were topped with feather ticks now house the tools of an artisan. Within reach of the workbench are all the usual hammers, routers, chisels, patterns, and so forth. The visitor can sense the sifting of sawdust and wood shavings from the workbench to the floor. His display areas are no longer open to the public.

Among the items A. T. Berger has created for the pleasure of the *Kinder* are wooden trains and cars, miniature horse-drawn sleighs, rocking horses, flared wooden bells with metal liners and clappers, candy-dispensing machines, and children's furniture. He has an especially fine sense of humor that can be perceived in some of his creations, and he frequently has a nice little story to enhance the intrigue that the toy holds.

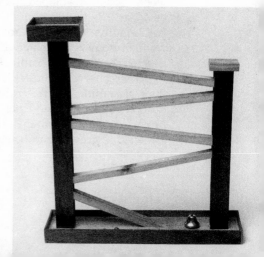

The Klickerbahn *has been a popular marble game in the seven villages for many generations. Many are created by craftsmen; others are fashioned by individuals who do woodworking as a hobby. (Courtesy, Amana Heritage Society)*

As a very caring and kind person, this teacher, toy maker, rural mail carrier, and poet would often leave a poem in the mailbox of an ailing fellow Inspirationist to extend a word of cheer and his good wishes. One such poem was simply titled "You."

> You have an eye for beauty,
> You have music in your soul,
> You have compassion for your fellow man,
> You have the will that says "I am."
> You have the guidance from above
> To assist you in your tasks of love
> With all of these in times that try men's souls.
> Be assured my friend
> That you will reach
> Most of your cherished goals.

Berger Custom Woodwork Shop

Just off U.S. Highway 151 north of Amana is a privately owned, family-operated cabinet shop that specializes in custom furniture and a wide selection of walnut, cherry, and oak gift and decorator items. In addition, Dean Berger and his wife, Donna, have done other kinds of interesting and unusual projects, such as making a replacement dashboard for a 1922 Studebaker touring car, building and installing new window frames in an antique airplane, and constructing a steel guitar body.

The Berger Custom Woodwork Shop is on land that was once owned by the Amana Society. As is true with so many artisans of the area, Dean Berger, the son of a machinist and woodworker, developed his interest in working with wood as a boy. His family had a home workshop; he liked to use his imagination to design and build a variety of small wooden items. At the age of fifteen he started to work part time in the Amana Furniture Shop, where he was expected to do the chores of a novice—pile and load logs, sweep the floor, assemble chairs, crate furniture, and generally help others. Uncle Dan and Uncle Adolph, both Amana artisans, provided encouragement and guidance. As his skills and knowledge grew, Dean became a full-time employee of the

Amana Furniture Shop when Dan Berger was the manager. He worked for a time at the Krauss Furniture and Clock Factory and later became a postal employee.

In 1967 he opened his own cabinet shop. He had some new equipment, but much of the equipment he made himself with skills he had learned from his machinist father. Today he can fill almost any order with the tools and machines in his shop. He is also the proud owner of a sixteen-inch joiner that arrived in the Amanas in 1899.

Most of the cherry, walnut, and oak hardwoods used by the Bergers come from within a fifty- to one-hundred-mile radius of Amana. Some is purchased kiln-dried; that which is purchased green is air-dried or kiln-dried in a sawmill and lumbering operation in Belle Plaine, Iowa, a town about twenty miles to the west.

The Bergers use no stains on walnut and cherry woods. The varnish is applied by brush and hand sanded in the traditional Amana way; no polyurethanes are used. The soft and mellow glow of the finish is achieved by much hard work on the part of Donna Berger.

The shop carries a great variety of gift and decorator items, including footstools, wall shelves, wall lamps, sconces, knife holders, lazy Susans, barometers, pen holders, picture frames, hanging wine racks, and toy cars. Wall clocks are also available. Many items are reproductions of items found in Amana homes of an earlier day. A large portion of Berger-handcrafted items are sold in Amana gift shops and at gift and craft shows. Tourist business is good, with many buyers returning time after time to order additional items. Everything is guaranteed for workmanship and quality.

CHAPTER 11

Future Perspectives

The original Amana Society was a closely knit community in which church membership and communal living were the primary bonds. The only outsiders were laborers employed by the Society and a few visitors and tourists. The Change of 1932 initially retained much of the old, but gradually business development and social changes began to create new directions and dimensions. The Amana of today is not the "Amana that was and the Amana that is" as defined by Bertha Shambaugh's scholarly treatise on the subject.[1]

The Amana furniture industry expresses the nature of some of the changes that have taken place. From small beginnings this industry has flourished through growth and entrepreneurship. The structure of the industry today was probably not anticipated by the board that decided in 1932 to develop a furniture enterprise. In retrospect the growth of the industry portrays the vitality of capitalism and free enterprise. The Amana Furniture Shop became a major producer of fine furniture and significantly expanded its market through innovative techniques. In addition, Amana cabinetmakers, such as Dave Krauss and Norman Schanz, formed private businesses and enlarged the industry. Such growth would not have occurred under the old communal system.

182

A brick Amana home today.

The industry has been responsive to new technology, and there have been innovations in design. But the basic integrity of the old Amana furniture production and design has been retained. Christian Metz, as *Werkzeug,* Elder, and cabinetmaker, would be pleased with the Amana furniture of today and would view much of what is produced as familiar.

The future of the furniture industry seems secure. However, the number and size of enterprises within the industry are likely to change over time. A particular cabinet shop could experience significant economic growth or decline; bankruptcies and mergers are also possible. Entrepreneurship on the part of cabinetmakers and others will undoubtedly give rise to the entry of new firms.

The survival of individual enterprises involves more than the skills of the cabinetmaker. Such tasks as recruitment, training, and supervision can be highly strategic.

The use of electronic computers and other recently developed technologies is increasingly important. More effective marketing and financial planning offer other advantages.

These managerial responsibilities point to the need to make preparations for management succession. Family enterprises in particular should recognize that the new generation requires a good education and as much experience as possible in the performance of managerial tasks. A similar challenge exists for other enterprises faced with retirements in managerial ranks.

The furniture industry in the United States, of which the Amana industry is a part, can be divided into three categories. There are cabinet shops, such as these in Amana, where relatively few skilled craftsmen produce fine furniture with the extensive use of hand tools. Cabinet shops permit more diversity in design and can give customers a greater range of choice. However, the nature of traditional design, which characterizes Amana furniture, places limitations on diversity. There are also furniture factories that use semiautomatic equipment and considerable handwork to produce high-quality furniture. Finally, there are mass-production factories, which use equipment and techniques that permit quantity production at a relatively low cost.

The broader U.S. furniture industry is highly competitive, with frequent changes in the way in which furniture is marketed. For example, professional interior designers are playing an increasingly important role in the marketing of quality furniture. A related development is that larger numbers of people appreciate fine furniture and have the income to afford the best. Also important is that markets have become more international during recent years. These and other developments need to be given consideration in planning for the future.

The Amana furniture industry has customers throughout the United States and a few in foreign countries. Most of the cabinet shops do not plan a major expansion. There are advantages in remaining relatively small and highlighting the individual craftsman. Marketing is achieved through satisfied customers who show and tell others and through the thousands of people who visit Amana. For this reason the future of the furniture industry is related to the future of the Amana tourist industry. Visitors will continue to come so long as Amana remains as a distinct and unique historical entity. Highly important in this respect is the designation of the Amana colonies as a National Historic Preservation site. The Amana Heritage Museum makes a major contribution through its collection of books, dissertations, journal articles, maps, and photographs on the Community of True Inspiration. Most of the testimonies of the *Werkzeuge* from 1714 to 1883 are available for scholarly research. In addition, there are files containing data on births, deaths, and marriages; oral history tapes of interviews with more than one hundred members; and a comprehensive history of the Community of True Inspiration. The museum is staffed by Amana people who give guidance in using the collections and provide assistance in translating German texts. Amana people, especially young people, need to give explicit recognition to the significance of their original customs and traditions. Scholarly research and publications on the Amana past should always have a high priority.

The Amana Furniture Shop has an advantage in marketing through the Amana trade name. The privately owned cabinet shops are more restricted in their marketing potential. Their future is more closely related to Amana as a geographical place and historical-social entity. The use of the Amana trade name allows the potential to significantly expand production and marketing as well as to compete on a national, and even worldwide, basis with such quality furniture firms as Baker and Henredon.

The Amana of today has many dimensions. In some respects Amana is a geographical location in Iowa County, Iowa. Such a definition does not take into account the additional sites that have evolved since 1932. A sizable number of Amana business and tourist establishments can be found on Interstate 80, nine miles from Amana. A retail outlet for products of the Amana Society is located in Des Moines.

Amana Refrigeration, Inc., and its parent, the Raytheon Company, gave Amana an expanded dimension through use of the Amana trade name in marketing a diversity of manufactured products throughout the world. All of these must in some sense be included in what Amana is today.

Middle Amana and the Amana countryside today, with a view of the modern Amana Refrigeration, Inc., plant. The chimney in the lower right corner of the plant symbolizes a continuity with the Amana past. See photograph of the Amana woolen mill in 1910 on page 28. (Photographic Collection, Amana Refrigeration, Inc.)

Such private enterprises as those developed by Krauss, Schanz, Berger, and Kraft are also a part of Amana today, even though they are restricted in the use of the Amana trade name. Three of these have an Amana heritage that can be traced to Ebenezer and Hesse. Kraft does not have this heritage; yet he, his wife, and son have all been employed as craftspeople in Amana cabinet shops. In his own shop Kraft has continued to make fine furniture that follows the Amana tradition. It should be remembered that Amana has always been open to some outsiders. Religion was a primary test in the old days, but a further consideration was the need for certain skills.

There is a diversity of opinion on who should be included in the definition of Amana people. Some consider church membership an important criterion; others feel that although church attendance is highly recommended, the failure to do so does not mean a person is now an outsider. The ownership of Class A stock is another criterion; yet many who no longer own such stock are considered to be fully a part of Amana. Amana people who work for Amana-developed enterprises such as Amana Refrigeration, Inc., are generally included even though they may now live elsewhere. Should the spouse of an original Amana descendant or the children born to them be included in the definition of Amana? Most Amana people would not exclude them. Yet not all are equal in this respect.

As in other societies, some people are considered to have closer Amana ties than others. The descendants of the original families from Hesse are likely to have a more secure status than those who came into the fold at a later date. A waitress in one of the Amana restaurants expressed the importance of genealogy: "All of my grandparents were original Amana Society members; a grandfather was an Elder." A precise definition as to who are and who are not truly Amana may not be all that critical. What is important is an understanding of and a respect for the original Amana culture and heritage.

The governance of Amana has changed significantly through the years. Prior to 1932 the board of trustees and the Elders governed the religious and secular life of the Society. After the Change two boards were established, a board of trustees for the Amana Church Society and a board of directors for the secular Amana Society corporation. Governance began to change with the sale of what had been Society property to private individuals for business and personal purposes. Also important was a significant change in the residential population of the Amana villages. The Iowa Supreme Court gave explicit recognition to these changes by reducing the power of the Amana Board of Directors to regulate land use. The court emphasized that less than one-third of Amana residents are members of the Society. The

Iowa General Assembly addressed this matter through land-use legislation that gave voting rights to nonmember residents. Questions related to Class A stock are also important to future governance. These questions caused differences in 1972 and have implications for the future. However, a change in the articles of incorporation in 1989, giving the Amana Society perpetual corporate status under Iowa law, provides an improved basis for continuity and cooperation. Entrepreneurship on the part of Amana and other people will continue to reshape economic endeavor and business ownership.

Although the Amana church and business corporations will play a significant role, the changes noted above are likely to become more important in future Amana governance. However, the Amana heritage and traditions will be maintained through the efforts of the Amana people and the institutions they have developed for this purpose. More scholarly research and books are needed to give further emphasis to the importance of the past in viewing the future. Fine Amana furniture in many American homes will continue to express Amana history and tradition.

A German Submarine Brings Last Shipment of Dye

On July 9, 1916, the world's first commercial submarine made a four-thousand-mile trip across the Atlantic carrying shipments of German-made dye to America. The *Deutschland* of the North German line arrived unannounced on the east coast of the United States four miles south of Baltimore. The vessel was carrying no weapons of war, but both the event and the vessel caused much concern in Washington, D.C. The commander of the submarine, Captain Paul Koenig, had been able to successfully pass through earlier French and British blockades, much to their later astonishment. Detailing the perils of the trip, the captain described the sixteen-day voyage as the "daring trip of his craft across the Atlantic." Telling the reporters how his *Deutschland* played its game of hide and seek with the British navy, he said, "And we sat down upon the floor of the British channel because the roof was crowded with nosey destroyers, and we drank good French champagne while we sang, 'We've rings on our fingers and bells on our toes,' and presently the destroyers gave us room on the roof and we came up and went on to America. It was all just as

---

Information derived from personal interviews and a series of articles in *The Chicago Tribune*, July 10,11,12,14, 1916.

simple as that, I tell you." The submarine carried mostly dyes and chemicals, some of which were intended for final delivery and use at the Amana calico print mill. The war curtailed subsequent shipments of dye from Germany and woven cotton from the South. The business was forced to close in 1917. Captain Koenig made a personal visit to the Amanas in the 1930s.

Twenty-one Rules for the Examination of Our Daily Lives

I. Obey, without reasoning, God, and through God your superiors.

II. Study quiet, or serenity, within and without.

III. Within, to rule and master your thoughts.

IV. Without, to avoid all unnecessary words, and still to study silence and quiet.

V. Abandon self, with all its desires, knowledge and power.

VI. Do not criticize others, either for good or evil, neither to judge nor to imitate them; therefore contain yourself, remain at home, in the house and in your heart.

VII. Do not disturb your serenity or peace of mind—hence neither desire nor grieve.

VIII. Live in love and pity toward your neighbor, and indulge neither anger nor impatience in your spirit.

IX. Be honest, sincere, and avoid all deceit and even secretiveness.

X. Count every word, thought, and work done in the immediate presence of God, in sleeping and waking, eating, and drinking, etc., and give Him at once an account of it, to see if all is done in His fear and love.

XI. Be in all things sober, without levity or laughter; and without vain and idle words, works, or thoughts; much less heedless or idle.

Appendix B is reprinted from *Amana That Was and Amana That Is*, by Bertha H. M. Shambaugh (Iowa City: State Historical Society of Iowa, 1932), 234–44. Copyright 1932 State Historical Society of Iowa. Copyright renewed 1960. Reprinted by permission.

XII. Never think or speak of God without the deepest reverence, fear, and love, and therefore deal reverently with all spiritual things.

XIII. Bear all inner and outward sufferings in silence, complaining only to God; and accept all from Him in deepest reverence and obedience.

XIV. Notice carefully all that God permits to happen to you in your inner and outward life, in order that you may not fail to comprehend His will and to be led by it.

XV. Have nothing to do with unholy and particularly with needless business affairs.

XVI. Have no intercourse with worldly-minded men; never seek their society; speak little with them, and never without need; and then not without fear and trembling.

XVII. Therefore, what you have to do with such men do in haste; do not waste time in public places and worldly society, that you be not tempted and led away.

XVIII. Fly from the society of women-kind as much as possible, as a very highly dangerous magnet and magical fire.

XIX. Avoid obeisance and the fear of men; these are dangerous ways.

XX. Dinners, weddings, feasts, avoid entirely; at the best there is sin.

XXI. Constantly practice abstinence and temperance, so that you may be as wakeful after eating as before.

Twenty-four Rules for True Godliness

I. To tear all crude and subtle idols out of your hearts, that they may no longer befool you and mislead you further to idolatry against your God, so that His name be not defamed and He not suddenly go forth and avenge and save the glory of His name.

II. I desire that you shall have naught in common with the fruitless work of darkness; neither with grave sins and sinners, nor with the subtle within and without you. For what relationship and likeness has My holy temple with the temples of pride, unchasteness, ambition, seeking for power; and of the useless, superfluous, condemning prattling, which steals the time away from Me. How could the light unite with the darkness? How can you as children of the light unite with the ungodly, the liars and their works, the scoffers and blasphemers, who are nothing but darkness?

III. You shall henceforth in your external life conduct yourself so that those standing without find no longer cause for ill reports and for defaming My name. Suffer rather the wrong if you are abused. But above all flee from associations which hinder you from growing in godliness. All mockers and scoffers and those who recommend you unto vanity, you shall shun and have no dealings with them.

IV. You shall also perform your earthly task the longer the more according to the dictates of your conscience; and gladly desist from that which My spirit shows you to be sinful—not heeding your own loss, for I am the Lord, who can and will care and provide for the needs of your body—that through this you may not give cause for censure to the scoffer. The time which I still grant you here is very short; therefore, see to it well that My hand may bring forth and create within you a real harvest.

V. Let, I warn you, be far from you all falseness, lying, and hypocrisy. For I say unto you that I will give the spirit of discernment and will lay open unto you through the Spirit of Prophesy such vices. For to what end shall clay and metal be together? Would it not make for Me a useless vessel, which I could not use and should have to cast away with the rest. Behold, My children, I have chosen before many, many, many, and have promised to be unto you a fiery entrenchment against the defiance of your inner and outer enemies. Verily! Verily! I shall keep my promises, if only you endeavor to fulfil what you have promised and are promising.

VI. You shall therefore, none of you, strive for particular gifts and envy the one or the other to whom I give perchance the gift of prayer or maybe of wisdom. For such the enemy of My glory seeks ever to instill into you, especially the passionate and fickle souls, to impart to you thereby a poison destructive to the soul. You shall, all, all, all of you be filled with My pure and holy spirit when the time will come to pass, if you will let yourself be prepared in humility and patience according to My will. Then you too shall speak with tongues different from the tongues you now speak with. Then I shall be able to communicate with you most intimately.

VII. Put aside henceforth all backbiting, and all malice of the heart toward each other, which you have harbored hitherto! None of you are free from it! Behold I shall command the Spirit of my Love that He as often as you assemble in true simplicity of heart and in humility for prayer be in your very midst with His influence and may flow through the channels of His Love into the hearts He finds empty.

VIII. You must make yourself willing for all outer and inner suffering. For Belial will not cease to show unto you his rancor through his servants and through his invisible power. It is also pleasing to Me and absolutely necessary for you that you be tried through continuous sorrow, suffering, and cross, and be made firm and precious in My crucible. And he who does not dare (but none must be indolent himself in this) to exert all his physical and spiritual powers through My strength, let him depart that he may not be later a blemishing spot upon My glory.

IX. Do not lend in future your ears to suspicion and prejudice and take, because of your lack of self-knowledge, offence at each other where there is none. But each one among you shall become the mirror for the other. You shall, moreover, also endeavor to stand every day and hour before the Lord as a oneness, as a city or a light on a high mountain, which near and far shines bright and pure.

X. At the same time practice the longer the more outer and inner quiet. Seek ever, though it will be for the natural man which is inexperienced in this a hard death, to hide yourself in humility in the inner and undermost chamber of your nothingness, that I may bring in this soil to a befitting growth My seed which I have concealed therein.

XI. Behold, My people! I make with you this day a covenant which I bid you to keep faithfully and sacredly. I will daily wander amongst you and visit your place of rest, that I may see how you are disposed toward Me.

XII. Guard yourself. I, the Lord, warn you against indifference towards this covenant of grace and against negligence, indolence, and laziness which thus far have been for the most part your ruler and have controlled your heart. I shall not depart from your side nor from your midst, but shall Myself on the contrary reveal Myself ever more powerfully, holier, and more glorious through the light of My face in and among you, as long as you will bring forth to meet Me the honest and sincere powers of your will. This shall be the tie with which you can bind and hold Me. Behold I accept you this day as slaves of My will, as free-borns of My kingdom, as possessors of My heart! Therefore let yourself gladly and willingly be bound with the ties of My love, and the power of love shall never be wanting unto you.

XIII. And you who are the heads and fathers of households hear what I say unto you: The Lord has now chosen you as members of His Community with whom He desires to associate and dwell day by day. See, therefore, to this that you prove truly heads and lights of your households, which, however, always stand under their faithful head, your King; see that you may bring your helpmates to true conduct and fear of God through your own way of living, which you shall strive to make ever more faultless, more earnest and manly.

XIV. Your children, you who have any, you shall endeavor with all your power to sacrifice to Me and to lead to Me. I shall give you in abundance, if you only inwardly keep close to Me, wisdom, courage, understanding, bravery, and earnestness mingled with love, that you yourself may be able to live before them in the fear of

God and that your training may be blessed—that is, in those who want to submit to My hand in and through Me. But those who scorn you and do not heed my voice in and through you and otherwise, shall have their blood come upon their own heads. But you shall never abandon hope but wrestle for them with earnest prayer, struggle, and toil, which are the pangs of spiritual birth. But if you neglect them through indifference, negligence, half-heartedness, and laziness, then every such soul shall verily be demanded of such a father.

XV. Do now your part as I command you from without and frequently inwardly through My Spirit; do not desist, just as I never cease to work on you my disobedient children; then you will abide in my grace and save your souls. And such women and children shall bear the fruits of their sins as do not want to bow themselves under you and Me. I will henceforth no longer tolerate those grave offenses among you and in your houses about which the world and the children of wrath and disbelief have so much to say; but I have commanded the Spirit of My living breath, that He pass through all your houses and breathe upon every soul which does not wantonly close itself to Him. The dew of blessing shall flow from the blessed head of your high priest and prince of peace upon every male head among you, and through them it shall flow upon and into your helpmates, and through both man and wife into the offspring and children, so that all your seed shall be acceptable, pure, and holy before the Lord, since He has nourished and will nourish the same among you.

XVI. And none of your grown up children shall be permitted to attend your meetings, who have not previously received from their parents a good testimony according to the truth, not appearance, and without self-deception, as also from the Elders and leaders especially from the one who with his fellow workers has to watch over the training of the children, which is to be carried on with earnestness and love, but without all severity and harshness. This training is to be watched over with all earnestness; and should the parents be negligent and the case require it, so shall the latter be temporarily excluded (from the prayer-meetings) for their humiliation.

XVII. Prove yourselves as the people whom I have established for an eternal monument to Me, and whom I shall impress upon My heart as an eternal seal, so that the Spirit of My love may dwell upon you and within you, and work according to His desire.

XVIII. And this is the word which the Lord speaks of these strangers who so often visit you and cause so much disturbance: None, whom you find to be a scoffer, hypocrite, mocker, sneerer, derider, and unrepenting sinner, shall you admit to your Community and prayer-meetings. Once for all they are to be excluded that My refreshing dew and the shadow of My Love be never prevented from manifesting themselves among you. But if some should come to you with honest intentions who are not knowingly scoffers, hypocrites, and deriders, though it be one of those whom you call of the world, if he to your knowledge does not come with deceitful intentions, then you may well admit him. I shall give you My faithful servants and witnesses especially the spirit of discrimination and give you an exact feeling, whether they are sincere and come with honest intentions or otherwise.

XIX. If they then desire to visit you more frequently, you shall first acquaint them with your rules and ask them whether they will submit to these rules and to the test of the Elders. And then you shall read to them My laws and commands, which I give unto you; and if you see that they are earnestly concerned about their souls, then you shall gladly receive the weak, and become weak with them for a while, that is, you shall with them and for them repent and make their repentance your own. But if a scoffer or mocker declares that he repents, him you should only admit after considerable time and close scrutiny and examination of his conduct, if you find the latter to be righteous. For Satan will not cease to try to launch at you his fatal arrows through such people. Be therefore on your guard and watch that not the wolf come among you and scatter or even devour the sheep.

XX. And those who pledge themselves with hand and mouth after the aforesaid manner to you shall make public profession before the Community and also make an open confession of their resolve, and I shall indeed show you if this latter comes from the hearts; the conduct of those you shall watch closely, whether they live according to their profession and promise or not, lest the dragon defile your garments with his drivel.

XXI. (To the Elders.) Thus My Elder and his fellow-workers shall frequently visit the members of the Community and see how things are in their homes and how it stands about their hearts. I shall give to you my servant (E. L. Gruber) and to your Brothers keen eyes, if you only pray for it. And if you find that one is in uncalled sadness, or lives in negligence, impudence, boisterousness, or the like, then you shall admonish him in love. If he repents you shall rejoice. But if after repeated admonition he does not mend his ways, then you shall put him to shame openly before the Community; and if even this does not help then you shall exclude him for a while. Yet I shall ever seek my sheep, those who are already excluded and those who in the future because of their own guilt must be excluded, and I shall ever try to lead them in their nothingness into my pasture.

XXII. And to all of you I still give this warning: Let none of you reject brotherly admonition and punishment, so that secret pride grows not like a poisonous thorn in such a member and torment and poison his whole heart.

XXIII. You shall not form a habit of anything of the external exercises (forms of worship) and the duties committed to you, or I shall be compelled to forbid them again; on the contrary, you shall make your meetings ever more fervent, more earnest, more zealous, in the true simple love towards each other, fervent and united in Me, the true Prince of Peace.

XXIV. This the members and brethren of the Community shall sincerely and honestly pledge with hand and mouth to my Elders, openly in the assembly, after they have carefully considered it, and it shall be kept sacred ever after.

Managers of the Amana Furniture Shop after 1932

1932–1940 (?) AUGUST FRANKE, in charge of furniture-making

1932–1934 JOHN NOE, in charge of business aspects of furniture shop and assisted in sales; developed a product catalog

1940–1951 JAKE ZSCHERNY, manager of total operation

1940–1944 THEO KIPPENHAN, assisted management with special emphasis on sales

1951–1956 DAVE KRAUSS, manager of total operation

1956–1958 DAN BERGER, manager of total operation

1958–1967 DAN BERGER, primarily responsible for furniture production

1967–1985 RALPH ZUBER, production manager

1958–1988 MARVIN BENDORF, sales manager

1985–present LEE HERR, production manager

1988–1989 BERT RAMSEY, manager of total operation

1989–present DAVID RETTIG, sales manager

During the years in which there were both a sales manager and a production manager, each would report directly to the Society board.

Notes

Chapter 1: Introduction

1. Alan Gowans, *Images of American Living* (New York: J. B. Lippincott, 1964), 14.

Chapter 2: Historical Background

1. William Rufus Perkins and Barthinius L. Wick, *History of the Amana Society*, Historical Monograph no. 1 (Iowa City: University of Iowa, 1891), 3. Charles F. Noe relates the early history of the Inspirationists and subsequent events in *A Brief History of the Amana Society, 1714–1900* (Amana, Iowa: 1904). Somewhat later, Henry G. Moershel, who was the president of the Amana Church Society, wrote an interesting summary of the beginnings of the Inspirationists published in a booklet, *The Amana Colonies* (Monticello, Iowa: Julin Printing Co., 1969). It contains a variety of topics assembled by Joan Liffring Zug and John Zug.

2. Perkins and Wick, *History of the Amana Society*, 10.

3. Bertha M. H. Shambaugh, *Amana That Was and Amana That Is* (Iowa City: State Historical Society of Iowa, 1932), 24.

4. Francis Alan DuVal, "Christian Metz, German-American Religious Leader and Pioneer" (Ph.D. diss., University of Iowa, 1948), 34.

5. Perkins and Wick, *History of the Amana Society*, 17.

6. Frank J. Lankes, *The Ebenezer Community of True Inspiration* (Gardenville, N.Y.: published by author, 1949), 4.

7. DuVal gives the birthdate as 1793: DuVal, "Christian Metz," 49, as verified in the *Kirchenbuch* of Neuwied, DuVal, "Christian Metz," 84, n. 2. Shambaugh, *Amana That Was and Amana That Is*, 41. Shambaugh and others have recorded 1794 as Metz's birthdate.

8. DuVal, "Christian Metz," 66.

9. Frank J. Lankes, *The Ebenezer Society*, Pt. 3 (West Seneca, N.Y.: West Seneca Historical Society, 1963), 21.

10. DuVal, "Christian Metz," 103–4.

11. DuVal, "Christian Metz," 128.

12. In the 1850 federal census, Metz reported himself as an Elder.

13. Clair Watson, "The Amana Style in Architecture," in *The Iowan Visits Amana* (Shenandoah, Iowa: Sentinel Publishing Co., 1954, 1959), 10.

14. Shambaugh, *Amana That Was and Amana That Is*, 64.

15. DuVal, "Christian Metz," 150–54. The journey to Kansas is described in the *Neun und zwanzigste Sammlung* (1854), 244–51. *Sammlungen* containing the testimonies of Christian Metz and

Barbara Heinemann, often with a brief description of the setting in which they occurred, can be found in yearbooks in the German language, *Jahrbücher der wahren Inspirations-Gemeinden oder Bezeugungen des Geistes des Herrn*, published in Hesse, Ebenezer, and Amana. Some of the testimonies of Rock and other earlier *Werkzeuge* have also been published.

16. Perkins and Wick, *History of the Amana Society*, 53.

17. Perkins and Wick, *History of the Amana Society*, 54.

18. *Neun und zwanzigste Sammlung*, 277.

19. 1856 Iowa County Deed Records, bk. 5, 262, 263; and bk. 6, 96, 97.

20. James C. Dinwiddie, *History of Iowa County Iowa and Its People*, vol. 1 (Chicago: S. J. Clarke Publishing Co., 1915), 72–73. This source provides a good historical background of life in early Iowa County in which the Amana Society settled in the 1850s. Another pertinent book is *Pioneer Recollections* (Cedar Rapids, Iowa: The Historical Publishing Co., 1941), compiled by Harley Ransom.

21. Lankes, *The Ebenezer Community of True Inspiration*, 80–81.

22. Perkins and Wick, *History of the Amana Society*, 55.

23. Barbara Hoehnle, *Utilitarian Woodwork of the Amana Colonies*, vol. 5 of Amana, Iowa, Art and Craft Series, Amana Arts Guild (n.d., pages not numbered).

24. Marjorie Wightman, "The Amana Story," in *The Iowan Visits Amana* (Shenandoah, Iowa: Sentinel Publishing Co., 1954, 1959), 3.

25. *Dreissigste Sammlung, 1855* (Amana, 1868), 162.

26. *Dreissigste Sammlung, 1855*, 201.

27. In 1823, Barbara Heinemann married George Landmann, which caused her to lose her God-given gift as a *Werkzeug* for a number of years. However, her maiden name is used throughout this book.

28. The testimonies spoken or written by the *Werkzeuge* are printed in *Jahrbücher* which date from 1714 to 1883. See note 15.

Chapter 3: The Amana Villages

1. Today the United States Post Office officially recognizes West, High, and Middle as the full names of these towns, with no postal listing for East and Upper South. Only South Amana and Amana retain the name Amana in their mailing addresses.

2. Designs for fabric were small overall geometric or stylized floral patterns.

3. Charles G. Parsons, "A Valuation of the Industrial Property of the Amana Society" (Master's thesis, Iowa State College, Ames, 1932), 22.

4. In 1875, the Society had 2,775 head of sheep, which produced 169,470 pounds of wool for the mills. *Census of Iowa, 1875* (Des Moines: State Printer, 1875), 277.

5. Elizabeth M. Schoenfelder, "Tenacious Lily," *The Iowan*, 2, no. 5 (June–July, 1954): 20, 51, 52.

6. Bertha M. H. Shambaugh, *Amana That Was and Amana That Is* (Iowa City: State Historical Society of Iowa, 1932), 310, n. 89. Shambaugh wrote that a priest from one of the nearby towns would gather large quantities of ripe seeds from the lotus lilies each fall. The seeds are round, of medium size, and have a glossy surface. They were used for making rosaries.

7. Emilie Hoppe, "The Journey to Amana: 'The End Makes Clear the Start,' " *Willkommen*, 8, no. 2 (Spring 1989): 14. The sawmill in High Amana was one that had been dismantled and transported from Ebenezer in 1857 to facilitate erecting buildings.

8. Clair Watson, "The Amana Style in Architecture," in *The Iowan Visits Amana*, (Shenandoah, Iowa: Sentinel Publishing Co., 1954, 1959), 11.

9. Robert Edwin Clark, *A Cultural and Historical Geography of the Amana Colony, Iowa* (Lincoln: University of Nebraska, 1974), 97. Nogging is the use of wood blocks or common bricks placed between studs. In the Amana homes brick without mortar was used as an insulating material.

10. Ruth G. Snyder, "The Arts and Crafts of the Amana Society" (Master's thesis, University of Iowa, 1949), 18.

11. Meals for children under two years of age and the incapacitated elderly were carried in baskets to the homes.

12. A cord of wood measures four feet by four feet by eight feet. The pieces of wood for the heating stoves were cut into sixteen-inch lengths.

13. Land and Community Associates, *Culture and Environment: A Challenge for the Amana Colonies—An Inventory and Plan Prepared for the Amana Colonies, Iowa County, Iowa* (Charlottesville, Va., 1977), 26.

Chapter 4: The Amana Society: 1855-1932

1. Bertha M. H. Shambaugh, *Amana That Was and Amana That Is* (Iowa City: State Historical Society of Iowa, 1932), 105.

2. Shambaugh, *Amana That Was and Amana That Is*, 95-96.

3. Shambaugh, *Amana That Was and Amana That Is*, 103.

4. Shambaugh, *Amana That Was and Amana That Is*, 102-3.

5. James C. Dinwiddie, *History of Iowa County, Iowa, and Its People*, vol. 1 (Chicago: S. J. Clarke Publishing Co., 1915), 53, 219.

6. See Chap. 2, n. 15.

7. Charles Nordhoff, *The Communistic Societies of the United States* (1875; reprint, New York: Dover Publications, 1966), 55.

8. Shambaugh, *Amana That Was and Amana That Is*, 245-46.

9. Sandra Van Amburg, "Long Ago Christmas: She Wished for a Bicycle; Got a Rocking Chair," *Cedar Rapids Gazette*, Oct. 5, 1975, 11B.

10. A bride wore a black bridal gown, similar to the traditional black dress, with a lace cap, shawl, and apron until about 1953. After this date, the brides started to wear white. The ceremony now includes musical accompaniment and bridesmaids.

11. Charles Nordhoff, *Communistic Societies*, 36. Contrary to most sources, Nordhoff relates that the solemn wedding ceremony was held at the home of the bride's father, with the parents and several Elders present. After words of wisdom, prayer, hymns, and a simple supper, all would go to their respective homes.

12. Francis Alan DuVal, "Christian Metz, German-American Religious Leader and Pioneer" (Ph.D. diss., University of Iowa, 1948), 211.

13. DuVal, "Christian Metz," 210.

Chapter 5: Furniture in Early Amana Life

1. Helen Comstock, *American Furniture* (New York: Viking Press, 1962), 130.

2. It is believed that these chairs were purchased from a firm located in Burlington, Iowa. No old records or invoices could be located.

3. Charles Van Ravenswaay, *Drawn from Nature: The Botanical Art of Joseph Prestele and His Sons* (Washington, D.C.: Smithsonian Institution Press, 1984). This is an interesting and nicely illustrated book about the artists and their work.

4. Barbara Hoehnle, *Utilitarian Woodwork of the Amana Colonies*, vol. 5 of Amana, Iowa, Art and Craft Series, Amana Arts Guild. (n.d., pages not numbered).

5. Van Ravenswaay, *Drawn from Nature*, 43.

6. Bill Zuber's fame sprouted in an onion field! A scout from the Cleveland Indians had heard about Zuber's pitching skill. He traveled to Amana to visit Bill, who, at the time, was helping with the Amana onion harvest. With no baseball immediately available the scout selected a firm baseball-sized onion, handed it to the seventeen-year-old, and asked him to throw it toward a distant barn. Zuber threw it over the barn. He subsequently pitched for the Cleveland Indians, Washington Senators, Boston Red Sox, and New York Yankees.

Chapter 6: Furniture Design

1. Grace E. Chaffee, "An Analysis of Sectarian Community Culture with Especial Reference to the Amana Society," *Antiques*, August 1929, 114.

2. Frank J. Lankes, *The Ebenezer Community of True Inspiration* (Gardenville, N.Y.: published by author, 1949), 7. Lankes described the travels of Christian Metz and his group of four, who were searching for new lands that would be appropriate for the Community of True Inspiration.

3. Chaffee, "Analysis of Sectarian Community Culture," 118.

4. Mabel Munson Swan, "Moravian Cabinetmakers of a Piedmont Craft Center," *Antiques*, June 1951, 456.

Chapter 7: The Cabinetmaker in Communal Amana

1. Unless otherwise noted, data in this chapter were obtained from interviews of selected members of the Amana Society and compiled by the author.
2. John Ruskin, *The Seven Lamps of Architecture* (London: J. M. Dent and Sons, 1921), 54. Ruskin, an early spokesman of modern design philosophy, urged a return to honest craftsmanship, particularly that of earlier periods when hand craftsmanship was an integral part of design. See Nikolaus Pevsner, *Pioneers of Modern Design from William Morris to Walter Gropius* (New York: Museum of Modern Art, 1949).
3. One man in each cabinet shop was the supervisor and reported directly to the Elders.
4. The cabinetmaker interviewed could not identify "whitewood" by specie; however, in general terms whitewood refers to a light-colored wood, such as butternut.

Chapter 8: The Clockmaker

1. Carl J. Bendorf made a presentation entitled "Frederick Hahn: Amana Craftsman and Clockmaker" on July 16, 1986, at the Amana Heritage Museum. Bendorf, a skilled clockmaker, is a member of the Amana Society and has conducted much research on the life and contributions of Hahn.

Chapter 9: From Communal Living to Capitalism

1. Lawrence L. Rettig, *Amana Today* (South Amana, Iowa, 1975), 4. This book contains a vast amount of significant factual source material.
2. *Census of Iowa for 1880* (Des Moines: State Printer, 1883), 506.
3. James C. Dinwiddie, *History of Iowa County Iowa and Its People*, vol. 1 (Chicago: S. J. Clarke Publishing Co., 1915), 73.
4. *Census of Iowa for 1880*, 506.
5. Francis Alan DuVal, "Christian Metz, German-American Religious Leader and Pioneer" (Ph.D. diss., University of Iowa, 1948), 212.
6. DuVal, "Christian Metz," 173.
7. DuVal, "Christian Metz," 173. Metz used the words "*Unlauterkeiten und Buhlereien.*"
8. DuVal, "Christian Metz," 199.
9. Rettig, *Amana Today*, 7.
10. Adam Smith, *The Wealth of Nations*, Cannan edition (1776; reprint New York: Modern Library, 1937), 423.

11. *The Christian Century*, 52, no. 39 (September 25, 1935): 1212.

12. Members of this group included Dr. Carl Noe, Dr. Henry G. Moershel, William Miller, Peter Stuck, and William Ehrle. Rettig, *Amana Today*, 12.

13. Arthur Barlow, *Recollections . . . The Amana Society's Great Change* (privately published, 1971), 6.

14. For a comprehensive account of the controversy relating to Class A stock and other matters, see Rettig, *Amana Today*, 75-88.

15. Rettig, *Amana Today*, 172-79, includes a copy of the Amana Church Society constitution and bylaws.

16. Rettig, *Amana Today*, 61.

17. Rettig, *Amana Today*, 22.

18. *Amana Society Bulletin* 5, no. 2 (March 30, 1933): 1-2.

19. Barlow, *Recollections*. Much of the factual background is derived from this source. Barlow's experiences as business manager during the transition period were discussed in private conversations prior to his death in 1983.

20. Charles G. Parsons, "A Valuation of the Industrial Property of the Amana Society" (Master's thesis, Iowa State College, Ames, 1932), 33.

21. Barlow, *Recollections*, 5.

22. Barlow, *Recollections*, 13.

23. Rettig, *Amana Today*, 37.

24. Rettig, *Amana Today*, 25.

25. For different versions of how this business developed, see Barlow, *Recollections*, 22-23, and Rettig, *Amana Today*, 43-45.

26. *Amana Society v. Colony Inn, Inc., et al*, Iowa 315 N.W. 2nd, 101 (St. Paul, Minn.: West Publishing Co., 1982).

27. Iowa 315 N.W. 2nd, 118.

28. *Laws of the Seventieth General Assembly of the State of Iowa*, regular sess., 1983, Chap. 108, 188-94.

29. Iowa 315 N.W. 2nd, 119.

Chapter 10: The Amana Furniture Industry

1. After the Change in 1932, the people of Amana continued to call the Amana cabinet shop by that name; the name officially became the Amana Furniture Shop in the 1950s.

2. Louise Ade Boger, *Furniture Past and Present* (Garden City, N.Y.: Doubleday Co., 1966), 470.

3. "Wooten: King of Desks," *The Antique Trader Annual of Articles*, vol. 5, 1976, 55.

Chapter 11: Future Perspectives

1. Bertha M. H. Shambaugh, *Amana That Was and Amana That Is* (Iowa City: State Historical Society of Iowa, 1932).

Selected Readings

The books listed below are good sources for individuals who want to know more about Amana. Those who want to delve more deeply into the history of the Inspirationists may wish to make use of the references in the notes. Scholars should take advantage of the Museum of Amana History research library located in Amana, Iowa. The collection contains books (including three hundred children's books), dissertations, journal articles, family histories, business and personal ledgers, maps, oral history tapes, photographs, testimonies of the *Werkzeuge* (mostly in German), and miscellaneous items such as diaries, letters, and manuscripts (primarily in old German script).

Andelson, Jonathon. "Communalism and Change in the Amana Society, 1855–1932." Ph.D. diss., University of Michigan, 1974.

Barthel, Diane L. *Amana: From Pietist Sect to American Community.* Lincoln, Nebr.: University of Nebraska Press, 1984.

Clark, Robert Edwin. "A Cultural and Historical Geography of the Amana Colony, Iowa." Ph.D. diss., University of Nebraska-Lincoln, 1974.

A Collection of Traditional Amana Recipes. Homestead, Iowa: Ladies Auxiliary, Homestead Welfare Club, 1948.

DuVal, Francis Alan. "Christian Metz, German-American Religious Leader and Pioneer." Ph.D. diss., University of Iowa, 1948.

Lankes, Frank James. *The Ebenezer Community of True Inspiration.* Buffalo, N.Y.: Kiesling Publishing Co., 1949.

_____. *The Ebenezer Society.* West Seneca, N.Y.: West Seneca Historical Society, 1963.

Nordhoff, Charles. *The Communistic Societies of the United States.* 1875. Reprint, New York: Dover Publications, 1966.

The Palimpsest 52, no. 4 (April 1971). This issue, consisting of essays by a number of persons and numerous photographs, is entirely devoted to Amana.

Perkins, William Rufus, and Barthinius L. Wick. *History of the Amana Society.* Iowa City: University of Iowa, 1891.

Rettig, Lawrence. *Amana Today.* South Amana, Iowa, 1975.

Schanz, Joanna E. *Willow Basketry of the Amana Colonies.* Iowa City, Iowa: Penfield Press, 1986.

Shambaugh, Bertha M. H. *Amana That Was and Amana That Is.* Iowa City: The State Historical Society of Iowa, 1932. The first part of this book is a reprint of *Amana; The Community of True Inspiration*, first published in 1908, which was reprinted by the Penfield Press, Iowa City, Iowa, in 1988 with the sponsorship of the Museum of Amana History and the State Historical Society.

Van Ravenswaay, Charles. *Drawn From Nature: The Botanical Art of Joseph Prestele and His Sons*. Washington, D.C.: Smithsonian Institution Press, 1984.

Yambura, Barbara S., and Eunice Willis Bodine. *A Change and A Parting: My Story of Amana*. Ames: Iowa State University Press, 1960.

Index

Page numbers in **bold** refer to illustrations.

207